C-693   CAREER EXAMINATION SERIES

*This is your
PASSBOOK for...*

Recreation Supervisor

*Test Preparation Study Guide
Questions & Answers*

COPYRIGHT NOTICE

This book is SOLELY intended for, is sold ONLY to, and its use is RESTRICTED to individual, bona fide applicants or candidates who qualify by virtue of having seriously filed applications for appropriate license, certificate, professional and/or promotional advancement, higher school matriculation, scholarship, or other legitimate requirements of education and/or governmental authorities.

This book is NOT intended for use, class instruction, tutoring, training, duplication, copying, reprinting, excerption, or adaptation, etc., by:

1) Other publishers
2) Proprietors and/or Instructors of "Coaching" and/or Preparatory Courses
3) Personnel and/or Training Divisions of commercial, industrial, and governmental organizations
4) Schools, colleges, or universities and/or their departments and staffs, including teachers and other personnel
5) Testing Agencies or Bureaus
6) Study groups which seek by the purchase of a single volume to copy and/or duplicate and/or adapt this material for use by the group as a whole without having purchased individual volumes for each of the members of the group
7) Et al.

Such persons would be in violation of appropriate Federal and State statutes.

PROVISION OF LICENSING AGREEMENTS – Recognized educational, commercial, industrial, and governmental institutions and organizations, and others legitimately engaged in educational pursuits, including training, testing, and measurement activities, may address request for a licensing agreement to the copyright owners, who will determine whether, and under what conditions, including fees and charges, the materials in this book may be used them. In other words, a licensing facility exists for the legitimate use of the material in this book on other than an individual basis. However, it is asseverated and affirmed here that the material in this book CANNOT be used without the receipt of the express permission of such a licensing agreement from the Publishers. Inquiries re licensing should be addressed to the company, attention rights and permissions department.

All rights reserved, including the right of reproduction in whole or in part, in any form or by any means, electronic or mechanical, including photocopying, recording, or by any information storage and retrieval system, without permission in writing from the Publisher.

Copyright © 2024 by
National Learning Corporation

212 Michael Drive, Syosset, NY 11791
(516) 921-8888 • www.passbooks.com
E-mail: info@passbooks.com

PUBLISHED IN THE UNITED STATES OF AMERICA

PASSBOOK® SERIES

THE *PASSBOOK® SERIES* has been created to prepare applicants and candidates for the ultimate academic battlefield – the examination room.

At some time in our lives, each and every one of us may be required to take an examination – for validation, matriculation, admission, qualification, registration, certification, or licensure.

Based on the assumption that every applicant or candidate has met the basic formal educational standards, has taken the required number of courses, and read the necessary texts, the *PASSBOOK® SERIES* furnishes the one special preparation which may assure passing with confidence, instead of failing with insecurity. Examination questions – together with answers – are furnished as the basic vehicle for study so that the mysteries of the examination and its compounding difficulties may be eliminated or diminished by a sure method.

This book is meant to help you pass your examination provided that you qualify and are serious in your objective.

The entire field is reviewed through the huge store of content information which is succinctly presented through a provocative and challenging approach – the question-and-answer method.

A climate of success is established by furnishing the correct answers at the end of each test.

You soon learn to recognize types of questions, forms of questions, and patterns of questioning. You may even begin to anticipate expected outcomes.

You perceive that many questions are repeated or adapted so that you can gain acute insights, which may enable you to score many sure points.

You learn how to confront new questions, or types of questions, and to attack them confidently and work out the correct answers.

You note objectives and emphases, and recognize pitfalls and dangers, so that you may make positive educational adjustments.

Moreover, you are kept fully informed in relation to new concepts, methods, practices, and directions in the field.

You discover that you are actually taking the examination all the time: you are preparing for the examination by "taking" an examination, not by reading extraneous and/or supererogatory textbooks.

In short, this PASSBOOK®, used directedly, should be an important factor in helping you to pass your test.

RECREATION SUPERVISOR

DUTIES:
Under the general supervision of the Superintendent of Recreation or a higher level administrator, an incumbent of this class has specific responsibility for the organization, administration, planning, promotion, development, coordination, training and supervision of one or more major segments of the recreation and/or parks department programs. This includes responsibility for agency-wide recreation programs and operations in specified localities, in a specialty activity, or, for operating services of a general type, i.e., playgrounds, recreation centers, mobile recreation units, roving leaders, or counseling services, outdoor recreation, special population groups, athletics and sports, aquatics, arts and crafts, cultural arts, drama, dance, etc. with reference to their general scope and to specific applications. A Recreation Supervisor may be expected to spend some time in a leadership role for particular programs and activities. Supervision, either direct or general, is exercised over subordinate professional, paraprofessional, clerical and seasonal personnel. Does related work as required.

SUBJECT OF EXAMINATION:
The written test will be designed to test for knowledge, skills, and/or abilities in such areas as:

1. **Principles and practices of leisure recreation** - These questions test for a knowledge of the basic concepts and common practices employed in the planning and implementation of leisure-time recreation programs in athletics, social activities, and avocational interests. Questions may cover such areas as program/activity planning for the major user groups, program/activity planning for people with special needs; operation of recreation areas, recreation center buildings, and specialized recreation facilities (pools, tennis courts, etc.); and scheduling of activities.

2. **Preparing written material** - These questions test for the ability to present information clearly and accurately, and to organize paragraphs logically and comprehensibly. For some questions, you will be given information in two or three sentences followed by four restatements of the information. You must then choose the best version. For other questions, you will be given paragraphs with their sentences out of order. You must then choose, from four suggestions, the best order for the sentences.

3. **Recreation administration** - These questions test for knowledge and application of the principles and practices of recreation administration as they relate to structuring and maintaining a recreation program. Questions may cover such topics as planning (forecasting, identification of objectives, etc.); organizing (identification and grouping of work tasks, definition and delegation of responsibility and authority, establishment of relationships, etc.); control (development and implementation of standards, evaluation techniques, etc.); and policy formulation (information systems, evaluation of alternatives, etc.).

4. **Working with people to facilitate recreation and/or leisure activities** - These questions will test for the knowledge and abilities necessary to work with individuals of all backgrounds in the context of providing recreation and leisure activities. Questions may cover such areas as: human behavior and development, handling difficult situations, engaging and motivating participants, building rapport with participants, working with volunteers, and planning appropriate activities for participant group.

5. **Supervision** - These questions test for knowledge of the principles and practices employed in planning, organizing, and controlling the activities of a work unit toward predetermined objectives. The concepts covered, usually in a situational question format, include such topics as assigning and reviewing work; evaluating performance; maintaining work standards; motivating and developing subordinates; implementing procedural change; increasing efficiency; and dealing with problems of absenteeism, morale, and discipline.

HOW TO TAKE A TEST

I. YOU MUST PASS AN EXAMINATION

A. *WHAT EVERY CANDIDATE SHOULD KNOW*

Examination applicants often ask us for help in preparing for the written test. What can I study in advance? What kinds of questions will be asked? How will the test be given? How will the papers be graded?

As an applicant for a civil service examination, you may be wondering about some of these things. Our purpose here is to suggest effective methods of advance study and to describe civil service examinations.

Your chances for success on this examination can be increased if you know how to prepare. Those "pre-examination jitters" can be reduced if you know what to expect. You can even experience an adventure in good citizenship if you know why civil service exams are given.

B. *WHY ARE CIVIL SERVICE EXAMINATIONS GIVEN?*

Civil service examinations are important to you in two ways. As a citizen, you want public jobs filled by employees who know how to do their work. As a job seeker, you want a fair chance to compete for that job on an equal footing with other candidates. The best-known means of accomplishing this two-fold goal is the competitive examination.

Exams are widely publicized throughout the nation. They may be administered for jobs in federal, state, city, municipal, town or village governments or agencies.

Any citizen may apply, with some limitations, such as the age or residence of applicants. Your experience and education may be reviewed to see whether you meet the requirements for the particular examination. When these requirements exist, they are reasonable and applied consistently to all applicants. Thus, a competitive examination may cause you some uneasiness now, but it is your privilege and safeguard.

C. *HOW ARE CIVIL SERVICE EXAMS DEVELOPED?*

Examinations are carefully written by trained technicians who are specialists in the field known as "psychological measurement," in consultation with recognized authorities in the field of work that the test will cover. These experts recommend the subject matter areas or skills to be tested; only those knowledges or skills important to your success on the job are included. The most reliable books and source materials available are used as references. Together, the experts and technicians judge the difficulty level of the questions.

Test technicians know how to phrase questions so that the problem is clearly stated. Their ethics do not permit "trick" or "catch" questions. Questions may have been tried out on sample groups, or subjected to statistical analysis, to determine their usefulness.

Written tests are often used in combination with performance tests, ratings of training and experience, and oral interviews. All of these measures combine to form the best-known means of finding the right person for the right job.

II. HOW TO PASS THE WRITTEN TEST

A. NATURE OF THE EXAMINATION

To prepare intelligently for civil service examinations, you should know how they differ from school examinations you have taken. In school you were assigned certain definite pages to read or subjects to cover. The examination questions were quite detailed and usually emphasized memory. Civil service exams, on the other hand, try to discover your present ability to perform the duties of a position, plus your potentiality to learn these duties. In other words, a civil service exam attempts to predict how successful you will be. Questions cover such a broad area that they cannot be as minute and detailed as school exam questions.

In the public service similar kinds of work, or positions, are grouped together in one "class." This process is known as *position-classification*. All the positions in a class are paid according to the salary range for that class. One class title covers all of these positions, and they are all tested by the same examination.

B. FOUR BASIC STEPS

1) Study the announcement

How, then, can you know what subjects to study? Our best answer is: "Learn as much as possible about the class of positions for which you've applied." The exam will test the knowledge, skills and abilities needed to do the work.

Your most valuable source of information about the position you want is the official exam announcement. This announcement lists the training and experience qualifications. Check these standards and apply only if you come reasonably close to meeting them.

The brief description of the position in the examination announcement offers some clues to the subjects which will be tested. Think about the job itself. Review the duties in your mind. Can you perform them, or are there some in which you are rusty? Fill in the blank spots in your preparation.

Many jurisdictions preview the written test in the exam announcement by including a section called "Knowledge and Abilities Required," "Scope of the Examination," or some similar heading. Here you will find out specifically what fields will be tested.

2) Review your own background

Once you learn in general what the position is all about, and what you need to know to do the work, ask yourself which subjects you already know fairly well and which need improvement. You may wonder whether to concentrate on improving your strong areas or on building some background in your fields of weakness. When the announcement has specified "some knowledge" or "considerable knowledge," or has used adjectives like "beginning principles of…" or "advanced … methods," you can get a clue as to the number and difficulty of questions to be asked in any given field. More questions, and hence broader coverage, would be included for those subjects which are more important in the work. Now weigh your strengths and weaknesses against the job requirements and prepare accordingly.

3) Determine the level of the position

Another way to tell how intensively you should prepare is to understand the level of the job for which you are applying. Is it the entering level? In other words, is this the position in which beginners in a field of work are hired? Or is it an intermediate or advanced level? Sometimes this is indicated by such words as "Junior" or "Senior" in the class title. Other jurisdictions use Roman numerals to designate the level – Clerk I, Clerk II, for example. The word "Supervisor" sometimes appears in the title. If the level is not indicated by the title, check the description of duties. Will you be working under very close supervision, or will you have responsibility for independent decisions in this work?

4) Choose appropriate study materials

Now that you know the subjects to be examined and the relative amount of each subject to be covered, you can choose suitable study materials. For beginning level jobs, or even advanced ones, if you have a pronounced weakness in some aspect of your training, read a modern, standard textbook in that field. Be sure it is up to date and has general coverage. Such books are normally available at your library, and the librarian will be glad to help you locate one. For entry-level positions, questions of appropriate difficulty are chosen – neither highly advanced questions, nor those too simple. Such questions require careful thought but not advanced training.

If the position for which you are applying is technical or advanced, you will read more advanced, specialized material. If you are already familiar with the basic principles of your field, elementary textbooks would waste your time. Concentrate on advanced textbooks and technical periodicals. Think through the concepts and review difficult problems in your field.

These are all general sources. You can get more ideas on your own initiative, following these leads. For example, training manuals and publications of the government agency which employs workers in your field can be useful, particularly for technical and professional positions. A letter or visit to the government department involved may result in more specific study suggestions, and certainly will provide you with a more definite idea of the exact nature of the position you are seeking.

III. KINDS OF TESTS

Tests are used for purposes other than measuring knowledge and ability to perform specified duties. For some positions, it is equally important to test ability to make adjustments to new situations or to profit from training. In others, basic mental abilities not dependent on information are essential. Questions which test these things may not appear as pertinent to the duties of the position as those which test for knowledge and information. Yet they are often highly important parts of a fair examination. For very general questions, it is almost impossible to help you direct your study efforts. What we can do is to point out some of the more common of these general abilities needed in public service positions and describe some typical questions.

1) General information

Broad, general information has been found useful for predicting job success in some kinds of work. This is tested in a variety of ways, from vocabulary lists to questions about current events. Basic background in some field of work, such as sociology or economics, may be sampled in a group of questions. Often these are principles which have become familiar to most persons through exposure rather than through formal training. It is difficult to advise you how to study for these questions; being alert to the world around you is our best suggestion.

2) Verbal ability

An example of an ability needed in many positions is verbal or language ability. Verbal ability is, in brief, the ability to use and understand words. Vocabulary and grammar tests are typical measures of this ability. Reading comprehension or paragraph interpretation questions are common in many kinds of civil service tests. You are given a paragraph of written material and asked to find its central meaning.

3) Numerical ability
Number skills can be tested by the familiar arithmetic problem, by checking paired lists of numbers to see which are alike and which are different, or by interpreting charts and graphs. In the latter test, a graph may be printed in the test booklet which you are asked to use as the basis for answering questions.

4) Observation
A popular test for law-enforcement positions is the observation test. A picture is shown to you for several minutes, then taken away. Questions about the picture test your ability to observe both details and larger elements.

5) Following directions
In many positions in the public service, the employee must be able to carry out written instructions dependably and accurately. You may be given a chart with several columns, each column listing a variety of information. The questions require you to carry out directions involving the information given in the chart.

6) Skills and aptitudes
Performance tests effectively measure some manual skills and aptitudes. When the skill is one in which you are trained, such as typing or shorthand, you can practice. These tests are often very much like those given in business school or high school courses. For many of the other skills and aptitudes, however, no short-time preparation can be made. Skills and abilities natural to you or that you have developed throughout your lifetime are being tested.

Many of the general questions just described provide all the data needed to answer the questions and ask you to use your reasoning ability to find the answers. Your best preparation for these tests, as well as for tests of facts and ideas, is to be at your physical and mental best. You, no doubt, have your own methods of getting into an exam-taking mood and keeping "in shape." The next section lists some ideas on this subject.

IV. KINDS OF QUESTIONS

Only rarely is the "essay" question, which you answer in narrative form, used in civil service tests. Civil service tests are usually of the short-answer type. Full instructions for answering these questions will be given to you at the examination. But in case this is your first experience with short-answer questions and separate answer sheets, here is what you need to know:

1) Multiple-choice Questions
Most popular of the short-answer questions is the "multiple choice" or "best answer" question. It can be used, for example, to test for factual knowledge, ability to solve problems or judgment in meeting situations found at work.

A multiple-choice question is normally one of three types—
- It can begin with an incomplete statement followed by several possible endings. You are to find the one ending which *best* completes the statement, although some of the others may not be entirely wrong.
- It can also be a complete statement in the form of a question which is answered by choosing one of the statements listed.

- It can be in the form of a problem – again you select the best answer.

Here is an example of a multiple-choice question with a discussion which should give you some clues as to the method for choosing the right answer:

When an employee has a complaint about his assignment, the action which will *best* help him overcome his difficulty is to
  A. discuss his difficulty with his coworkers
  B. take the problem to the head of the organization
  C. take the problem to the person who gave him the assignment
  D. say nothing to anyone about his complaint

In answering this question, you should study each of the choices to find which is best. Consider choice "A" – Certainly an employee may discuss his complaint with fellow employees, but no change or improvement can result, and the complaint remains unresolved. Choice "B" is a poor choice since the head of the organization probably does not know what assignment you have been given, and taking your problem to him is known as "going over the head" of the supervisor. The supervisor, or person who made the assignment, is the person who can clarify it or correct any injustice. Choice "C" is, therefore, correct. To say nothing, as in choice "D," is unwise. Supervisors have and interest in knowing the problems employees are facing, and the employee is seeking a solution to his problem.

2) True/False Questions

The "true/false" or "right/wrong" form of question is sometimes used. Here a complete statement is given. Your job is to decide whether the statement is right or wrong.

SAMPLE: A roaming cell-phone call to a nearby city costs less than a non-roaming call to a distant city.

This statement is wrong, or false, since roaming calls are more expensive.

This is not a complete list of all possible question forms, although most of the others are variations of these common types. You will always get complete directions for answering questions. Be sure you understand *how* to mark your answers – ask questions until you do.

V. RECORDING YOUR ANSWERS

Computer terminals are used more and more today for many different kinds of exams.

For an examination with very few applicants, you may be told to record your answers in the test booklet itself. Separate answer sheets are much more common. If this separate answer sheet is to be scored by machine – and this is often the case – it is highly important that you mark your answers correctly in order to get credit.

An electronic scoring machine is often used in civil service offices because of the speed with which papers can be scored. Machine-scored answer sheets must be marked with a pencil, which will be given to you. This pencil has a high graphite content which responds to the electronic scoring machine. As a matter of fact, stray dots may register as answers, so do not let your pencil rest on the answer sheet while you are pondering the correct answer. Also, if your pencil lead breaks or is otherwise defective, ask for another.

Since the answer sheet will be dropped in a slot in the scoring machine, be careful not to bend the corners or get the paper crumpled.

The answer sheet normally has five vertical columns of numbers, with 30 numbers to a column. These numbers correspond to the question numbers in your test booklet. After each number, going across the page are four or five pairs of dotted lines. These short dotted lines have small letters or numbers above them. The first two pairs may also have a "T" or "F" above the letters. This indicates that the first two pairs only are to be used if the questions are of the true-false type. If the questions are multiple choice, disregard the "T" and "F" and pay attention only to the small letters or numbers.

Answer your questions in the manner of the sample that follows:

32. The largest city in the United States is
    A. Washington, D.C.
    B. New York City
    C. Chicago
    D. Detroit
    E. San Francisco

1) Choose the answer you think is best. (New York City is the largest, so "B" is correct.)
2) Find the row of dotted lines numbered the same as the question you are answering. (Find row number 32)
3) Find the pair of dotted lines corresponding to the answer. (Find the pair of lines under the mark "B.")
4) Make a solid black mark between the dotted lines.

VI. BEFORE THE TEST

Common sense will help you find procedures to follow to get ready for an examination. Too many of us, however, overlook these sensible measures. Indeed, nervousness and fatigue have been found to be the most serious reasons why applicants fail to do their best on civil service tests. Here is a list of reminders:

- Begin your preparation early – Don't wait until the last minute to go scurrying around for books and materials or to find out what the position is all about.
- Prepare continuously – An hour a night for a week is better than an all-night cram session. This has been definitely established. What is more, a night a week for a month will return better dividends than crowding your study into a shorter period of time.
- Locate the place of the exam – You have been sent a notice telling you when and where to report for the examination. If the location is in a different town or otherwise unfamiliar to you, it would be well to inquire the best route and learn something about the building.
- Relax the night before the test – Allow your mind to rest. Do not study at all that night. Plan some mild recreation or diversion; then go to bed early and get a good night's sleep.
- Get up early enough to make a leisurely trip to the place for the test – This way unforeseen events, traffic snarls, unfamiliar buildings, etc. will not upset you.
- Dress comfortably – A written test is not a fashion show. You will be known by number and not by name, so wear something comfortable.

- Leave excess paraphernalia at home – Shopping bags and odd bundles will get in your way. You need bring only the items mentioned in the official notice you received; usually everything you need is provided. Do not bring reference books to the exam. They will only confuse those last minutes and be taken away from you when in the test room.
- Arrive somewhat ahead of time – If because of transportation schedules you must get there very early, bring a newspaper or magazine to take your mind off yourself while waiting.
- Locate the examination room – When you have found the proper room, you will be directed to the seat or part of the room where you will sit. Sometimes you are given a sheet of instructions to read while you are waiting. Do not fill out any forms until you are told to do so; just read them and be prepared.
- Relax and prepare to listen to the instructions
- If you have any physical problem that may keep you from doing your best, be sure to tell the test administrator. If you are sick or in poor health, you really cannot do your best on the exam. You can come back and take the test some other time.

VII. AT THE TEST

The day of the test is here and you have the test booklet in your hand. The temptation to get going is very strong. Caution! There is more to success than knowing the right answers. You must know how to identify your papers and understand variations in the type of short-answer question used in this particular examination. Follow these suggestions for maximum results from your efforts:

1) Cooperate with the monitor

The test administrator has a duty to create a situation in which you can be as much at ease as possible. He will give instructions, tell you when to begin, check to see that you are marking your answer sheet correctly, and so on. He is not there to guard you, although he will see that your competitors do not take unfair advantage. He wants to help you do your best.

2) Listen to all instructions

Don't jump the gun! Wait until you understand all directions. In most civil service tests you get more time than you need to answer the questions. So don't be in a hurry. Read each word of instructions until you clearly understand the meaning. Study the examples, listen to all announcements and follow directions. Ask questions if you do not understand what to do.

3) Identify your papers

Civil service exams are usually identified by number only. You will be assigned a number; you must not put your name on your test papers. Be sure to copy your number correctly. Since more than one exam may be given, copy your exact examination title.

4) Plan your time

Unless you are told that a test is a "speed" or "rate of work" test, speed itself is usually not important. Time enough to answer all the questions will be provided, but this does not mean that you have all day. An overall time limit has been set. Divide the total time (in minutes) by the number of questions to determine the approximate time you have for each question.

5) Do not linger over difficult questions
   If you come across a difficult question, mark it with a paper clip (useful to have along) and come back to it when you have been through the booklet. One caution if you do this – be sure to skip a number on your answer sheet as well. Check often to be sure that you have not lost your place and that you are marking in the row numbered the same as the question you are answering.

6) Read the questions
   Be sure you know what the question asks! Many capable people are unsuccessful because they failed to *read* the questions correctly.

7) Answer all questions
   Unless you have been instructed that a penalty will be deducted for incorrect answers, it is better to guess than to omit a question.

8) Speed tests
   It is often better NOT to guess on speed tests. It has been found that on timed tests people are tempted to spend the last few seconds before time is called in marking answers at random – without even reading them – in the hope of picking up a few extra points. To discourage this practice, the instructions may warn you that your score will be "corrected" for guessing. That is, a penalty will be applied. The incorrect answers will be deducted from the correct ones, or some other penalty formula will be used.

9) Review your answers
   If you finish before time is called, go back to the questions you guessed or omitted to give them further thought. Review other answers if you have time.

10) Return your test materials
   If you are ready to leave before others have finished or time is called, take ALL your materials to the monitor and leave quietly. Never take any test material with you. The monitor can discover whose papers are not complete, and taking a test booklet may be grounds for disqualification.

VIII. EXAMINATION TECHNIQUES

1) Read the general instructions carefully. These are usually printed on the first page of the exam booklet. As a rule, these instructions refer to the timing of the examination; the fact that you should not start work until the signal and must stop work at a signal, etc. If there are any *special* instructions, such as a choice of questions to be answered, make sure that you note this instruction carefully.

2) When you are ready to start work on the examination, that is as soon as the signal has been given, read the instructions to each question booklet, underline any key words or phrases, such as *least, best, outline, describe* and the like. In this way you will tend to answer as requested rather than discover on reviewing your paper that you *listed without describing*, that you selected the *worst* choice rather than the *best* choice, etc.

3) If the examination is of the objective or multiple-choice type – that is, each question will also give a series of possible answers: A, B, C or D, and you are called upon to select the best answer and write the letter next to that answer on your answer paper – it is advisable to start answering each question in turn. There may be anywhere from 50 to 100 such questions in the three or four hours allotted and you can see how much time would be taken if you read through all the questions before beginning to answer any. Furthermore, if you come across a question or group of questions which you know would be difficult to answer, it would undoubtedly affect your handling of all the other questions.

4) If the examination is of the essay type and contains but a few questions, it is a moot point as to whether you should read all the questions before starting to answer any one. Of course, if you are given a choice – say five out of seven and the like – then it is essential to read all the questions so you can eliminate the two that are most difficult. If, however, you are asked to answer all the questions, there may be danger in trying to answer the easiest one first because you may find that you will spend too much time on it. The best technique is to answer the first question, then proceed to the second, etc.

5) Time your answers. Before the exam begins, write down the time it started, then add the time allowed for the examination and write down the time it must be completed, then divide the time available somewhat as follows:
   - If 3-1/2 hours are allowed, that would be 210 minutes. If you have 80 objective-type questions, that would be an average of 2-1/2 minutes per question. Allow yourself no more than 2 minutes per question, or a total of 160 minutes, which will permit about 50 minutes to review.
   - If for the time allotment of 210 minutes there are 7 essay questions to answer, that would average about 30 minutes a question. Give yourself only 25 minutes per question so that you have about 35 minutes to review.

6) The most important instruction is to *read each question* and make sure you know what is wanted. The second most important instruction is to *time yourself properly* so that you answer every question. The third most important instruction is to *answer every question*. Guess if you have to but include something for each question. Remember that you will receive no credit for a blank and will probably receive some credit if you write something in answer to an essay question. If you guess a letter – say "B" for a multiple-choice question – you may have guessed right. If you leave a blank as an answer to a multiple-choice question, the examiners may respect your feelings but it will not add a point to your score. Some exams may penalize you for wrong answers, so in such cases *only*, you may not want to guess unless you have some basis for your answer.

7) Suggestions
   a. Objective-type questions
      1. Examine the question booklet for proper sequence of pages and questions
      2. Read all instructions carefully
      3. Skip any question which seems too difficult; return to it after all other questions have been answered
      4. Apportion your time properly; do not spend too much time on any single question or group of questions

5. Note and underline key words – *all, most, fewest, least, best, worst, same, opposite*, etc.
6. Pay particular attention to negatives
7. Note unusual option, e.g., unduly long, short, complex, different or similar in content to the body of the question
8. Observe the use of "hedging" words – *probably, may, most likely*, etc.
9. Make sure that your answer is put next to the same number as the question
10. Do not second-guess unless you have good reason to believe the second answer is definitely more correct
11. Cross out original answer if you decide another answer is more accurate; do not erase until you are ready to hand your paper in
12. Answer all questions; guess unless instructed otherwise
13. Leave time for review

  b. Essay questions
    1. Read each question carefully
    2. Determine exactly what is wanted. Underline key words or phrases.
    3. Decide on outline or paragraph answer
    4. Include many different points and elements unless asked to develop any one or two points or elements
    5. Show impartiality by giving pros and cons unless directed to select one side only
    6. Make and write down any assumptions you find necessary to answer the questions
    7. Watch your English, grammar, punctuation and choice of words
    8. Time your answers; don't crowd material

8) Answering the essay question

Most essay questions can be answered by framing the specific response around several key words or ideas. Here are a few such key words or ideas:

M's: manpower, materials, methods, money, management
P's: purpose, program, policy, plan, procedure, practice, problems, pitfalls, personnel, public relations

  a. Six basic steps in handling problems:
    1. Preliminary plan and background development
    2. Collect information, data and facts
    3. Analyze and interpret information, data and facts
    4. Analyze and develop solutions as well as make recommendations
    5. Prepare report and sell recommendations
    6. Install recommendations and follow up effectiveness

  b. Pitfalls to avoid
    1. *Taking things for granted* – A statement of the situation does not necessarily imply that each of the elements is necessarily true; for example, a complaint may be invalid and biased so that all that can be taken for granted is that a complaint has been registered

2. *Considering only one side of a situation* – Wherever possible, indicate several alternatives and then point out the reasons you selected the best one
3. *Failing to indicate follow up* – Whenever your answer indicates action on your part, make certain that you will take proper follow-up action to see how successful your recommendations, procedures or actions turn out to be
4. *Taking too long in answering any single question* – Remember to time your answers properly

IX. AFTER THE TEST

Scoring procedures differ in detail among civil service jurisdictions although the general principles are the same. Whether the papers are hand-scored or graded by machine we have described, they are nearly always graded by number. That is, the person who marks the paper knows only the number – never the name – of the applicant. Not until all the papers have been graded will they be matched with names. If other tests, such as training and experience or oral interview ratings have been given, scores will be combined. Different parts of the examination usually have different weights. For example, the written test might count 60 percent of the final grade, and a rating of training and experience 40 percent. In many jurisdictions, veterans will have a certain number of points added to their grades.

After the final grade has been determined, the names are placed in grade order and an eligible list is established. There are various methods for resolving ties between those who get the same final grade – probably the most common is to place first the name of the person whose application was received first. Job offers are made from the eligible list in the order the names appear on it. You will be notified of your grade and your rank as soon as all these computations have been made. This will be done as rapidly as possible.

People who are found to meet the requirements in the announcement are called "eligibles." Their names are put on a list of eligible candidates. An eligible's chances of getting a job depend on how high he stands on this list and how fast agencies are filling jobs from the list.

When a job is to be filled from a list of eligibles, the agency asks for the names of people on the list of eligibles for that job. When the civil service commission receives this request, it sends to the agency the names of the three people highest on this list. Or, if the job to be filled has specialized requirements, the office sends the agency the names of the top three persons who meet these requirements from the general list.

The appointing officer makes a choice from among the three people whose names were sent to him. If the selected person accepts the appointment, the names of the others are put back on the list to be considered for future openings.

That is the rule in hiring from all kinds of eligible lists, whether they are for typist, carpenter, chemist, or something else. For every vacancy, the appointing officer has his choice of any one of the top three eligibles on the list. This explains why the person whose name is on top of the list sometimes does not get an appointment when some of the persons lower on the list do. If the appointing officer chooses the second or third eligible, the No. 1 eligible does not get a job at once, but stays on the list until he is appointed or the list is terminated.

X. HOW TO PASS THE INTERVIEW TEST

The examination for which you applied requires an oral interview test. You have already taken the written test and you are now being called for the interview test – the final part of the formal examination.

You may think that it is not possible to prepare for an interview test and that there are no procedures to follow during an interview. Our purpose is to point out some things you can do in advance that will help you and some good rules to follow and pitfalls to avoid while you are being interviewed.

What is an interview supposed to test?

The written examination is designed to test the technical knowledge and competence of the candidate; the oral is designed to evaluate intangible qualities, not readily measured otherwise, and to establish a list showing the relative fitness of each candidate – as measured against his competitors – for the position sought. Scoring is not on the basis of "right" and "wrong," but on a sliding scale of values ranging from "not passable" to "outstanding." As a matter of fact, it is possible to achieve a relatively low score without a single "incorrect" answer because of evident weakness in the qualities being measured.

Occasionally, an examination may consist entirely of an oral test – either an individual or a group oral. In such cases, information is sought concerning the technical knowledges and abilities of the candidate, since there has been no written examination for this purpose. More commonly, however, an oral test is used to supplement a written examination.

Who conducts interviews?

The composition of oral boards varies among different jurisdictions. In nearly all, a representative of the personnel department serves as chairman. One of the members of the board may be a representative of the department in which the candidate would work. In some cases, "outside experts" are used, and, frequently, a businessman or some other representative of the general public is asked to serve. Labor and management or other special groups may be represented. The aim is to secure the services of experts in the appropriate field.

However the board is composed, it is a good idea (and not at all improper or unethical) to ascertain in advance of the interview who the members are and what groups they represent. When you are introduced to them, you will have some idea of their backgrounds and interests, and at least you will not stutter and stammer over their names.

What should be done before the interview?

While knowledge about the board members is useful and takes some of the surprise element out of the interview, there is other preparation which is more substantive. It *is* possible to prepare for an oral interview – in several ways:

1) Keep a copy of your application and review it carefully before the interview

This may be the only document before the oral board, and the starting point of the interview. Know what education and experience you have listed there, and the sequence and dates of all of it. Sometimes the board will ask you to review the highlights of your experience for them; you should not have to hem and haw doing it.

2) Study the class specification and the examination announcement

Usually, the oral board has one or both of these to guide them. The qualities, characteristics or knowledges required by the position sought are stated in these documents. They offer valuable clues as to the nature of the oral interview. For example, if the job involves supervisory responsibilities, the announcement will usually indicate that knowledge of modern supervisory methods and the qualifications of the candidate as a supervisor will be tested. If so, you can expect such questions, frequently in the form of a hypothetical situation which you are expected to solve. NEVER go into an oral without knowledge of the duties and responsibilities of the job you seek.

3) Think through each qualification required

Try to visualize the kind of questions you would ask if you were a board member. How well could you answer them? Try especially to appraise your own knowledge and background in each area, *measured against the job sought*, and identify any areas in which you are weak. Be critical and realistic – do not flatter yourself.

4) Do some general reading in areas in which you feel you may be weak

For example, if the job involves supervision and your past experience has NOT, some general reading in supervisory methods and practices, particularly in the field of human relations, might be useful. Do NOT study agency procedures or detailed manuals. The oral board will be testing your understanding and capacity, not your memory.

5) Get a good night's sleep and watch your general health and mental attitude

You will want a clear head at the interview. Take care of a cold or any other minor ailment, and of course, no hangovers.

What should be done on the day of the interview?

Now comes the day of the interview itself. Give yourself plenty of time to get there. Plan to arrive somewhat ahead of the scheduled time, particularly if your appointment is in the fore part of the day. If a previous candidate fails to appear, the board might be ready for you a bit early. By early afternoon an oral board is almost invariably behind schedule if there are many candidates, and you may have to wait. Take along a book or magazine to read, or your application to review, but leave any extraneous material in the waiting room when you go in for your interview. In any event, relax and compose yourself.

The matter of dress is important. The board is forming impressions about you – from your experience, your manners, your attitude, and your appearance. Give your personal appearance careful attention. Dress your best, but not your flashiest. Choose conservative, appropriate clothing, and be sure it is immaculate. This is a business interview, and your appearance should indicate that you regard it as such. Besides, being well groomed and properly dressed will help boost your confidence.

Sooner or later, someone will call your name and escort you into the interview room. *This is it*. From here on you are on your own. It is too late for any more preparation. But remember, you asked for this opportunity to prove your fitness, and you are here because your request was granted.

What happens when you go in?

The usual sequence of events will be as follows: The clerk (who is often the board stenographer) will introduce you to the chairman of the oral board, who will introduce you to the other members of the board. Acknowledge the introductions before you sit down. Do not be surprised if you find a microphone facing you or a stenotypist sitting by. Oral interviews are usually recorded in the event of an appeal or other review.

Usually the chairman of the board will open the interview by reviewing the highlights of your education and work experience from your application – primarily for the benefit of the other members of the board, as well as to get the material into the record. Do not interrupt or comment unless there is an error or significant misinterpretation; if that is the case, do not hesitate. But do not quibble about insignificant matters. Also, he will usually ask you some question about your education, experience or your present job – partly to get you to start talking and to establish the interviewing "rapport." He may start the actual questioning, or turn it over to one of the other members. Frequently, each member undertakes the questioning on a particular area, one in which he is perhaps most competent, so you can expect each member to participate in the examination. Because time is limited, you may also expect some rather abrupt switches in the direction the questioning takes, so do not be upset by it. Normally, a board member will not pursue a single line of questioning unless he discovers a particular strength or weakness.

After each member has participated, the chairman will usually ask whether any member has any further questions, then will ask you if you have anything you wish to add. Unless you are expecting this question, it may floor you. Worse, it may start you off on an extended, extemporaneous speech. The board is not usually seeking more information. The question is principally to offer you a last opportunity to present further qualifications or to indicate that you have nothing to add. So, if you feel that a significant qualification or characteristic has been overlooked, it is proper to point it out in a sentence or so. Do not compliment the board on the thoroughness of their examination – they have been sketchy, and you know it. If you wish, merely say, "No thank you, I have nothing further to add." This is a point where you can "talk yourself out" of a good impression or fail to present an important bit of information. Remember, *you close the interview yourself*.

The chairman will then say, "That is all, Mr. _____, thank you." Do not be startled; the interview is over, and quicker than you think. Thank him, gather your belongings and take your leave. Save your sigh of relief for the other side of the door.

How to put your best foot forward

Throughout this entire process, you may feel that the board individually and collectively is trying to pierce your defenses, seek out your hidden weaknesses and embarrass and confuse you. Actually, this is not true. They are obliged to make an appraisal of your qualifications for the job you are seeking, and they want to see you in your best light. Remember, they must interview all candidates and a non-cooperative candidate may become a failure in spite of their best efforts to bring out his qualifications. Here are 15 suggestions that will help you:

1) Be natural – Keep your attitude confident, not cocky

If you are not confident that you can do the job, do not expect the board to be. Do not apologize for your weaknesses, try to bring out your strong points. The board is interested in a positive, not negative, presentation. Cockiness will antagonize any board member and make him wonder if you are covering up a weakness by a false show of strength.

2) Get comfortable, but don't lounge or sprawl

Sit erectly but not stiffly. A careless posture may lead the board to conclude that you are careless in other things, or at least that you are not impressed by the importance of the occasion. Either conclusion is natural, even if incorrect. Do not fuss with your clothing, a pencil or an ashtray. Your hands may occasionally be useful to emphasize a point; do not let them become a point of distraction.

3) Do not wisecrack or make small talk

This is a serious situation, and your attitude should show that you consider it as such. Further, the time of the board is limited – they do not want to waste it, and neither should you.

4) Do not exaggerate your experience or abilities

In the first place, from information in the application or other interviews and sources, the board may know more about you than you think. Secondly, you probably will not get away with it. An experienced board is rather adept at spotting such a situation, so do not take the chance.

5) If you know a board member, do not make a point of it, yet do not hide it

Certainly you are not fooling him, and probably not the other members of the board. Do not try to take advantage of your acquaintanceship – it will probably do you little good.

6) Do not dominate the interview

Let the board do that. They will give you the clues – do not assume that you have to do all the talking. Realize that the board has a number of questions to ask you, and do not try to take up all the interview time by showing off your extensive knowledge of the answer to the first one.

7) Be attentive

You only have 20 minutes or so, and you should keep your attention at its sharpest throughout. When a member is addressing a problem or question to you, give him your undivided attention. Address your reply principally to him, but do not exclude the other board members.

8) Do not interrupt

A board member may be stating a problem for you to analyze. He will ask you a question when the time comes. Let him state the problem, and wait for the question.

9) Make sure you understand the question

Do not try to answer until you are sure what the question is. If it is not clear, restate it in your own words or ask the board member to clarify it for you. However, do not haggle about minor elements.

10) Reply promptly but not hastily

A common entry on oral board rating sheets is "candidate responded readily," or "candidate hesitated in replies." Respond as promptly and quickly as you can, but do not jump to a hasty, ill-considered answer.

11) Do not be peremptory in your answers

A brief answer is proper – but do not fire your answer back. That is a losing game from your point of view. The board member can probably ask questions much faster than you can answer them.

12) Do not try to create the answer you think the board member wants

He is interested in what kind of mind you have and how it works – not in playing games. Furthermore, he can usually spot this practice and will actually grade you down on it.

13) Do not switch sides in your reply merely to agree with a board member

Frequently, a member will take a contrary position merely to draw you out and to see if you are willing and able to defend your point of view. Do not start a debate, yet do not surrender a good position. If a position is worth taking, it is worth defending.

14) Do not be afraid to admit an error in judgment if you are shown to be wrong

The board knows that you are forced to reply without any opportunity for careful consideration. Your answer may be demonstrably wrong. If so, admit it and get on with the interview.

15) Do not dwell at length on your present job

The opening question may relate to your present assignment. Answer the question but do not go into an extended discussion. You are being examined for a *new* job, not your present one. As a matter of fact, try to phrase ALL your answers in terms of the job for which you are being examined.

Basis of Rating

Probably you will forget most of these "do's" and "don'ts" when you walk into the oral interview room. Even remembering them all will not ensure you a passing grade. Perhaps you did not have the qualifications in the first place. But remembering them will help you to put your best foot forward, without treading on the toes of the board members.

Rumor and popular opinion to the contrary notwithstanding, an oral board wants you to make the best appearance possible. They know you are under pressure – but they also want to see how you respond to it as a guide to what your reaction would be under the pressures of the job you seek. They will be influenced by the degree of poise you display, the personal traits you show and the manner in which you respond.

ABOUT THIS BOOK

This book contains tests divided into Examination Sections. Go through each test, answering every question in the margin. We have also attached a sample answer sheet at the back of the book that can be removed and used. At the end of each test look at the answer key and check your answers. On the ones you got wrong, look at the right answer choice and learn. Do not fill in the answers first. Do not memorize the questions and answers, but understand the answer and principles involved. On your test, the questions will likely be different from the samples. Questions are changed and new ones added. If you understand these past questions you should have success with any changes that arise. Tests may consist of several types of questions. We have additional books on each subject should more study be advisable or necessary for you. Finally, the more you study, the better prepared you will be. This book is intended to be the last thing you study before you walk into the examination room. Prior study of relevant texts is also recommended. NLC publishes some of these in our Fundamental Series. Knowledge and good sense are important factors in passing your exam. Good luck also helps. So now study this Passbook, absorb the material contained within and take that knowledge into the examination. Then do your best to pass that exam.

EXAMINATION SECTION

EXAMINATION SECTION
TEST 1

DIRECTIONS: Each question or incomplete statement is followed by several suggested answers or completions. Select the one that BEST answers the question or completes the statement. *PRINT THE LETTER OF THE CORRECT ANSWER IN THE SPACE AT THE RIGHT.*

1. In trying to improve the motivation of his subordinates, a recreation supervisor can achieve the BEST results by taking action based upon the assumption that most employees

    A. have an inherent dislike of work
    B. wish to be closely directed
    C. are more interested in security than in assuming responsibility
    D. will exercise self-direction without coercion

2. Recreation supervisors in public departments have many functions. Of the following, the function which is LEAST appropriate for a recreation supervisor is to

    A. serve as a deputy for the recreation administrator within his own district
    B. determine needs within his district and plan programs to meet these needs
    C. supervise, train, and evaluate all recreation personnel assigned to his district
    D. initiate and carry out fund-raising projects, such as bazaars and carnivals, to buy needed equipment

3. When there are conflicts or tensions between top management and lower-level employees in any public department, the supervisor should FIRST attempt to

    A. represent and enforce the management point of view
    B. act as the representative of the workers to get their ideas across to management
    C. serve as a two-way spokesman, trying to interpret each side to the other
    D. remain neutral, but keep informed of changes in the situation

4. A probationary period for new employees is usually provided in public agencies. The MAJOR purpose of such a period is *usually* to

    A. allow a determination of employee's suitability for the position
    B. obtain evidence as to employee's ability to perform in a higher position
    C. conform to requirements that ethnic hiring goals be met for all positions
    D. train the new employee in the duties of the position

5. An effective program of orientation for new employees usually includes all of the following EXCEPT

    A. having the supervisor introduce the new employee to his job, outlining his responsibilities and how to carry them out
    B. permitting the new worker to tour the facility or department, so he can observe all parts of it in action
    C. scheduling meetings for new employees, at which the job requirements are explained to them and they are given personnel manuals
    D. testing the new worker on his skills, and sending him to a centralized in-service workshop

6. In-service training is an important responsibility of recreation supervisors, either on a county or district-wide basis. The MAJOR reason for such training is to

   A. avoid future grievance procedures, because employees might say they were not prepared to carry out their jobs
   B. maximize the effectiveness of the department by helping each employee perform at his full potential
   C. satisfy inspection teams from central headquarters of the department
   D. help prevent disagreements with members of the community

7. There are many forms of useful in-service training. Of the following, the training method which is NOT an appropriate technique for recreation leadership development is to

   A. provide special workshops or clinics in activity skills
   B. conduct pre-season institutes to familiarize new workers with the program of the department and with their roles
   C. schedule team meetings for problem solving, including both supervisors and leaders
   D. have the leader rate himself on an evaluation form periodically

8. Of the following techniques of evaluating work training programs, the one that is BEST is to

   A. pass out a carefully designed questionnaire to the trainees at the completion of the program
   B. test the knowledge that trainees have both at the beginning of training and at its completion
   C. interview the trainees at the completion of the program
   D. evaluate performance before and after training for both a control group and an experimental group

9. Assume that a new supervisor is having difficulty making his instructions to subordinates clearly understood. The one of the following which is the FIRST step he should take in dealing with this problem is to

   A. set up a training workshop in communication skills
   B. determine the extent and nature of the communications gap
   C. repeat both verbal and written instructions several times
   D. simplify his written and spoken vocabulary

10. Discipline of employees is usually a supervisor's responsibility. There may be several useful forms of disciplinary action in public employment. Of the following, the form that is LEAST appropriate is the

    A. written reprimand or warning
    B. involuntary transfer to another work setting
    C. demotion or suspension
    D. assignment of added hours of work each week

11. Of the following, the MOST effective means of dealing with employee disciplinary problems is to

    A. give personality tests to individuals to identify their psychological problems
    B. distribute and discuss a policy manual containing exact rules governing employee behavior
    C. establish a single, clear penalty to be imposed for all wrongdoing irrespective of degree
    D. have supervisors get to know employees well through social mingling

12. A recently developed technique for appraising work performance is to have the supervisor record on a continual basis all significant incidents in each subordinate's behavior that indicate unsuccessful action and those that indicate poor behavior. Of the following, a major DISADVANTAGE of this method of performance appraisal is that it

    A. often leads to overly close supervision
    B. results in competition among those subordinates being evaluated
    C. tends to result in superficial judgments
    D. lacks objectivity for evaluating performance

13. Assume that you are a recreation supervisor and have observed the performance of an employee during a period of time. You have concluded that his performance needs improvement. In order to improve his performance, it would, therefore, be BEST for you to

    A. note your findings in the employee's personnel folder so that his behavior is a matter of record
    B. report the findings to the personnel officer so he can take prompt action
    C. schedule a problem solving conference with the employee
    D. recommend his transfer to simpler duties

14. When an employee's absences or latenesses seem to be nearing excessiveness, the supervisor should speak with him to find out what the problem is. Of the following, if such a discussion produces no reasonable explanation, the discussion usually BEST serves to

    A. affirm clearly the supervisor's adherence to proper policy
    B. alert other employees that such behavior in unacceptable
    C. demonstrate that the supervisor truly represents higher management
    D. notify the employee that his behavior is being observed and evaluated

15. Assume that an employee willfully and recklessly violates an important agency regulation. The nature of the violation is of such magnitude that it demands immediate action, but the facts of the case are not entirely clear. Further assume that the supervisor is free to make any of the following recommendations. The MOST appropriate action for the supervisor to take is to recommend that the employee be

    A. discharged   B. suspended
    C. forced to resign   D. transferred

16. Although employees' titles may be identical, each position in that title may be considerably different. Of the following, a supervisor should carefully assign each employee to a specific position based PRIMARILY on the employee's

    A. capability
    B. experience
    C. education
    D. seniority

17. The one of the following situations where it is MOST appropriate to transfer a recreation employee to a similar assignment is one in which the employee

    A. lacks motivation and interest
    B. experiences a personality conflict with his supervisor
    C. is negligent in the performance of his duties
    D. lacks capacity or ability to perform assigned tasks

18. The one of the following which is LEAST likely to be affected by improvements in the morale of recreation personnel is employee

    A. skill
    B. absenteeism
    C. turnover
    D. job satisfaction

19. The one of the following situations in which it is LEAST appropriate for a supervisor to delegate authority to subordinates is where the supervisor

    A. lacks confidence in his own abilities to perform certain work
    B. is overburdened and cannot handle all his responsibilities
    C. refers all disciplinary problems to his subordinate
    D. has to deal with an emergency or crisis

20. Of the following, the BEST attitude toward the use of volunteers in recreation programs is that volunteers should be

    A. discouraged, since they cannot be depended upon to show up regularly
    B. employed as a last resort when paid personnel are unavailable
    C. seen as an appropriate means of providing leadership, when effectively recruited and supervised
    D. eliminated to raise the professionalism of recreational personnel

21. A recreation supervisor finds that he is spending too much time on routine tasks, and not enough time on coordinating the work of his employees. It would be MOST advisable for this supervisor to

    A. delegate the task of work coordination to a capable subordinate
    B. eliminate some of the routine tasks that the unit is required to perform
    C. assign some of the routine tasks to his subordinates
    D. postpone the performance of routine tasks until he has achieved proper coordination of his employees' work

22. Of the following, the MOST important reason for having an office recreation manual in loose-leaf form rather than in permanent binding is that the loose-leaf form

    A. facilitates the addition of new material and the removal of obsolete material
    B. permits several people to use different sections of the manual at the same time
    C. is less expensive to prepare than permanent binding
    D. is more durable than permanent binding

23. In his first discussion with an employee newly appointed to the title of recreation assistant, the LEAST important of the following topics for a supervisor of a recreation unit to include is the

   A. duties the recreation assistant is expected to perform on the job
   B. functions of the unit
   C. methods of determining standards of recreational work performance
   D. nature and duration of the training the subordinate will receive on the job

24. A recreation supervisor has just been told by a subordinate, Mr. Jones, that another employee, Mr. Smith, deliberately disobeyed an important rule of the department by taking home some confidential departmental material. Of the following courses of action, it would be MOST advisable for the supervisor *first* to

   A. discuss the matter privately with both Mr. Jones and Mr. Smith at the same time
   B. call a meeting of the entire staff and discuss the matter generally without mentioning any employee by name
   C. arrange to supervise Mr. Smith's activities more closely
   D. discuss the matter privately with Mr. Smith

25. The one of the following actions which would be MOST efficient and economical for a recreation supervisor to take to minimize the effect of seasonal fluctuations in the work load of his unit is to

   A. increase his permanent staff until it is large enough to handle the work of the busy season
   B. request the purchase of time and labor saving equipment to be used primarily during the busy season
   C. lower, temporarily, the standards for quality of work performance during peak loads
   D. schedule for the slow season work that it is not essential to perform during the busy season

KEY (CORRECT ANSWERS)

1. D		11. B	
2. D		12. A	
3. C		13. C	
4. A		14. D	
5. D		15. B	
6. B		16. A	
7. D		17. B	
8. D		18. A	
9. B		19. C	
10. D		20. C	

21. C
22. A
23. C
24. D
25. D

TEST 2

DIRECTIONS: Each question or incomplete statement is followed by several suggested answers or completions. Select the one that BEST answers the question or completes the statement. *PRINT THE LETTER OF THE CORRECT ANSWER IN THE SPACE AT THE RIGHT.*

1. In most areas, winter programs are characterized by a heavier emphasis on each of the following EXCEPT 1.___
    A. social clubs
    B. instructional classes
    C. special events
    D. cultural activities

2. Of the following issues, which is MOST likely to be negotiated in a park and recreation labor union contractual agreement? 2.___
    A. Grievance procedures
    B. Fringe benefits
    C. Working conditions
    D. Seniority provisions

3. What type of legislation has been passed in certain states that permits two or more municipalities to establish joint park or recreation programs? 3.___
    A. Special recreation and park law
    B. Special district law
    C. Enabling law
    D. Home rule legislation

4. The National Recreation and Park Association recommends to all departments that a softball diamond be built for each _____ members of a community. 4.___
    A. 2000   B. 3000   C. 6000   D. 9000

5. At times, the performance of an individual staff member may call for discipline or corrective action – for example, a staff member may begin coming to work late. At the supervisory level, the initial corrective action for this type of behavior is typically 5.___
    A. a written reprimand, placed in the staff member's file
    B. a temporary suspension
    C. a verbal reprimand
    D. revocation of certain privileges

6. Which of the following statements about park and recreation volunteer workers is generally TRUE? 6.___
    A. They are a source of free help that will not create any expenditures for the agency.
    B. The volunteer program in an agency is not a separate, isolated element.
    C. With proper training, they can carry out any function that is carried out by professional staff.
    D. Volunteer effort is generally not as valuable to an agency as regular staff time.

7. Which of the following would be involved in an assessment of a manager's entrepreneurial skills? 7.___
    A. Proactivity
    B. Logical thought
    C. Perceptual objectivity
    D. Diagnostic use of concepts

8. When programming recreational activities for participants in early adulthood (20-39 years), it is important to remember that they do NOT generally

   A. have an interest in achieving specific and definite life goals
   B. become absorbed in interests and pursue them over extended periods of time
   C. experience a loss in fluid intelligence
   D. demonstrate competence independent of sex roles

9. In which of the following roles would a park and recreation manager typically exercise the most leadership?

   A. Maintaining recreation and park facilities
   B. Constructing leisure facilities
   C. Determining the community's needs for leisure facilities
   D. Designing recreation and park facilities

10. Typically, if a recreational activity or sports contest is cancelled or postponed by the recreation agency, the participants must be notified and consulted at LEAST _____ hours prior to the scheduled event.

    A. 4   B. 6   C. 24   D. 48

11. Strategic decisions that are made in determining the long-range direction an agency will follow, and which give direction to the organization, are described as _____ decisions.

    A. primary   B. problem-oriented
    C. reflex   D. task-oriented

12. For a park and recreation department, a systematic, carefully planned purchasing program must be based on each of the following elements EXCEPT

    A. careful attention to agency policy regarding classification of purchases
    B. familiarity with or access to sound legal advice
    C. compilation of an inventory of materials needed during the coming year, including a forecast of repair and replacement requirements
    D. a flexible purchasing policy statement that leaves the performance of suppliers open to interpretation

13. When programming recreational activities for participants in adolescence (13-19 years), it is important to remember that they do NOT generally

    A. possess mental perspectives regarding the past, present, and future
    B. have the ability to use inductive and deductive reasoning
    C. re-examine traditional values and attitudes
    D. have a mature self-concept

14. Under the _____ bond method of financing capital outlays, a government pays the bond purchaser a specified portion of the principal, plus interest, each year that the bond issue is in effect.

    A. term   B. serial
    C. callable   D. general obligation

15. The minimum area required for a public playground, excluding parking and natural scenic areas, is generally considered to be _____ acre(s).

    A. less than 1
    B. 6
    C. 15-25
    D. more than 30

16. Applied to leisure-service agencies, management guidelines that reflect major departmental principles in the provision of service, operation of facilities, management of personnel, or similar areas of management concern are referred to as

    A. policies
    B. target behaviors
    C. goals
    D. objectives

17. A task-oriented approach to leadership is most appropriate under each of the following conditions EXCEPT where

    A. the leader has legitimate power
    B. there is a competitive spirit among group members
    C. the leader is respected and trusted by group members
    D. the task is structured and clearly defined

18. Many public agencies rely on grants from both the public and private sectors in funding their departments. In recent years, the *lead time* from the early application for a grant and final delivery has increased to a period of about

    A. 6 months
    B. 18 months
    C. $2\frac{1}{2}$ years
    D. 4 months

19. A recreation programmer has designed a youth basketball tournament on a round-robin format. Which of the following is an advantage associated with this format?

    A. The emphasis is on maximum participation for an extended period of time.
    B. It is useful for a large number of participants.
    C. It does not require a large amount of facility utilization.
    D. It provides an *instant winner*.

20. In a recreation or park facility's on-season, an administrator wants to maintain a maximum level of care.
    Typically, how often should turf at the facility be watered?

    A. Daily
    B. Twice weekly
    C. Weekly
    D. Every two weeks

21. Which of the following is considered to be the responsibility of an administrative staff member at a park and recreation department?

    A. Coordinating the distribution of resources
    B. Developing personnel standards and procedures
    C. Supervising program-facility expenditures and fee collections
    D. Preparing budget proposals and annual reports

22. Which of the following steps in a park and recreation department's risk management procedure would generally be performed FIRST?

    A. Identifying actual risk occurrences and agency policies for handling them
    B. Determining appropriate methods of handling risks
    C. Identifying sources of potential risk
    D. Evaluating the probability of accidents and their probable degree of severity

23. Which of the following is NOT a benefit commonly associated with the use of volunteer workers at a park and recreation agency?

    A. Permitting the extension and enrichment of leisure services
    B. Assistance in interpreting the agency in the community
    C. Greater accountability than paid staff
    D. Contribution to favorable public relations

24. Generally, the FIRST step in a leisure service's managerial process is to

    A. determine informal agency processes
    B. prepare a policy manual
    C. establish organizational structures and operational codes
    D. decide upon the policies of the agency's directing function

25. A user of a recreational facility claims that he was injured while using the facility because a legally responsible staff member in the park and recreation department totally neglected his duty; the staff member did nothing to protect or assist the user. Specifically, the staff member is accused of liability due to

    A. negligence   B. nonfeasance
    C. misfeasance   D. malfeasance

KEY (CORRECT ANSWERS)

1.	C	11.	A
2.	B	12.	D
3.	B	13.	D
4.	B	14.	B
5.	C	15.	D
6.	B	16.	A
7.	A	17.	B
8.	D	18.	B
9.	C	19.	A
10.	C	20.	B

21.	B
22.	C
23.	C
24.	C
25.	B

EXAMINATION SECTION
TEST 1

DIRECTIONS: Each question or incomplete statement is followed by several suggested answers or completions. Select the one that BEST answers the question or completes the statement. *PRINT THE LETTER OF THE CORRECT ANSWER IN THE SPACE AT THE RIGHT.*

1. It has been said, *Leadership, more than areas and facilities, activities, and programs – important as they are – determines the success of municipal recreation service.* The BEST justification of this statement is that

    A. children learn more skills and at a faster rate with good leadership
    B. leadership can make facilities safe
    C. leadership gives deeper significance to the play of children
    D. the program is only as good as the leadership

    1.____

2. Changes or progress in our modern society have especially increased the need for recreation facilities of the type which provides

    A. development of friendships
    B. development of teamwork
    C. encouragement to creativeness
    D. individual and group competition

    2.____

3. The concept of recreation MOST generally accepted today is the _____ theory.

    A. instinct-practice
    B. recapitulation of culture-epochs
    C. self-expression
    D. surplus-energy

    3.____

4. The MOST serious danger of unsupervised play by children is that

    A. children learn many bad habits and acquire prejudices in their play when not supervised
    B. children playing by themselves are subject to greater hazards and potential injury
    C. misdirected play may lead to delinquency
    D. the unsupervised play environment may produce serious frustrations in children

    4.____

5. There are certain generally recognized principles of recreation programming for a community.
   The FULLEST statement of these principles is:

    A. A recreation plan for the community should result in the fullest use of all resources and be integrated with long-range planning for all other community services.
    B. Education for the worthy use of leisure in homes, schools, and other community institutions is essential.
    C. Opportunities and programs for recreation should be available twelve months of the year.
    D. All of the above

    5.____

6. Of the following functions, it is LEAST important for a recreation leader to

   A. develop a level of skill in children which will enable them to enjoy the activity
   B. develop winning teams
   C. maintain discipline and order
   D. provide opportunity for the greatest number to participate

7. The LEAST accurate of the following statements about the characteristics of a capable professional worker in the field of community activities is that he should have the ability to

   A. analyze thoughts and ideas in order to select basic usable concepts
   B. determine for himself, based upon his own professional experience and competence, the needs of the particular community activity
   C. express warmth of feeling in appropriate ways and without fear, as one basis for a sound relationship
   D. synthesize out of a mass of associations those which are significant and belong together in relation to a specific purpose

8. It is a GENERALLY accepted principle that volunteer leaders in a recreation program are valuable

   A. as long as they are willing to teach and direct activities without participating in them
   B. despite their need for constant supervision and guidance
   C. if they do not need constant supervision
   D. only if they possess a recreation skill

9. The MOST acceptable definition of discipline, according to the current theory of recreation, is:

   A. Methods used in special situations to achieve conformance to accepted patterns of behavior
   B. Punishment for those individuals or groups who violate legitimate rules or regulations which have been established for the general good
   C. The voluntary subordination of the individual to the welfare of the group
   D. Voluntary following of such rules as aid the development and integration of the individual

10. Motor skills are fundamental to all sports activity. It is MOST correct to say that motor skills

    A. are not generally found among pre-school children
    B. decrease in proportion to the decrease of strength and endurance with age
    C. once learned are never forgotten
    D. reach their highest state of development just after adolescence

11. From the viewpoint of professional recreation philosophy, the suggestion that two boys in disagreement should *put on the gloves* is

    A. *desirable;* it is a legitimate way of solving the disagreement
    B. *undesirable;* it assumes that the boy who wins is right in his views
    C. *undesirable;* it ignores the element of safety
    D. *undesirable;* it may involve the city in a lawsuit

12. Of the following, the BEST recreational approach to the problem of reducing juvenile delinquency is:

    A. Make recreational activities more demanding and satisfying than delinquent activities
    B. Provide a well-rounded community activities program and invite potential juvenile delinquents to join
    C. Provide children with a large enough place to play and with proper equipment and they will not get into trouble
    D. There is at present no reliable solution for juvenile delinquency; all we can hope to do is keep the good boys away from the bad

13. Studies of mental health and interest in hobbies have shown that

    A. interest in hobbies will keep a person mentally well
    B. the mentally well individual is less likely to have an interest in hobbies than the mentally ill person
    C. the mentally well individual is more likely to have an interest in hobbies than the mentally ill person
    D. there is no correlation between the two

14. The PRINCIPAL use to which a recreation leader should put a knowledge of common children's diseases is to

    A. give occasional advice to parents on safeguarding their children's health
    B. procure a medical history of the child in order to know the activities in which the child may participate
    C. recognize symptoms of conditions which may require medical care
    D. recognize symptoms of contagious diseases which require that a child be separated from the group

15. A child falls from a tree, hitting his head on the pavement below, knocking himself unconscious.
    The BEST first aid measures to take are:

    A. Apply a pressure bandage to prevent any bleeding and do not move the patient until the doctor arrives
    B. Avoid unnecessary handling and administer a mild stimulant when the child becomes conscious
    C. Do not move the patient but cover him with a coat or blanket until the doctor arrives
    D. Do not move the patient until the doctor arrives unless the patient demonstrates unusual lucidity and energy when he returns to consciousness

16. A thorough investigation should always be made of any accident occurring in a Park Department playground.
    The MAIN value of such an investigation is to

    A. demonstrate to the parents the interest which the Park Department takes in the care and safety of the children
    B. discover any factors that may be corrected which contributed to the accident

C. establish the extent to which Park Department employees may be responsible for the accident
D. provide a record of the accident so that the facts may be available in the event of a lawsuit

17. The MOST important of the following principles to consider in selecting games for a group is:

    A. Games should be adapted to the age-range, the number of members, and the various factors of difference represented in the group
    B. Games should be selected which are related to the cultural and ethnic backgrounds of the participants
    C. Games should not be complicated to teach, score, or perform
    D. The previous recreational experience of the participants should form the basis of selection

18. It is a common practice for playgrounds to conduct special events or celebrations at certain times.
    The MOST important principle which should guide planners of these events is:

    A. The regular program of the playground should be suspended, if necessary, in order to provide ample opportunity for practice
    B. They should be an outgrowth of the regular playground program
    C. They require much planning; hence, they should be scheduled at least six months in advance
    D. They should seldom be financed from the playground budget, but rather an outside sponsor should be sought

19. In basketball, when playing against a zone defense, the BEST strategy is

    A. set up weak side plays by overloading one side
    B. use a fast break
    C. use more dribbling than you would against a man-to-man defense
    D. utilize screens, quick cuts, and criss-cross breaks

20. In volleyball, the MOST effective method of passing, taking into account both control and power, is by having the

    A. arm kept rigid, the ball in direct contact with the palm of the hand, and snapping the wrist in the direction of the flight
    B. the fingers in contact with the ball, swinging the arm with a lifting motion
    C. heel of the hand in firm contact with the ball, swinging the arm with a lifting motion
    D. palm of the hand in direct contact with the ball, swinging the arm with a lifting motion

21. Generally speaking, it is good technique in batting in the game of softball to

    A. select a bat that feels rather heavy
    B. swing at all balls that come within reach
    C. swing the bat so that it is parallel to the ground at the moment of impact
    D. swing with all your might at the ball

22. The one of the following which is a rule of handball doubles is:

    A. A game is 25 points
    B. A *hinder* is called if a player drives a ball into an opponent and a point is credited to the side of the man who was hit
    C. If one partner swings at the ball and misses, the other partner is permitted to return the ball
    D. To keep the ball in play, it must be struck after hitting the wall and before hitting the ground

23. The activity which is especially useful with a large, cumbersome group of untutored individuals, as a lead-up activity to the production of a play, is

    A. answer-back story   B. Blackout
    C. Little Tom Tinker   D. puppet show

24. Analysis of the motion of a schottische dance shows the following sequence of fundamental steps:

    A. High brush step to the right side, close and transfer of weight left, and a hop left
    B. Step, step, close
    C. Three small runs followed by a hop
    D. Two hops, step, close, step

25. In recommending the purchase of playground equipment, a guiding principle should be that

    A. durability is usually at least as important as suitability
    B. equipment should be bought with a view to serving the largest number of participants
    C. good equipment, carefully selected, can largely substitute for leadership
    D. small areas should be loaded with apparatus

26. In introducing a game to a group unfamiliar with it, it is LEAST important that

    A. introductory instructions be brief
    B. the game be a simple one
    C. the game be stopped while interest is still high
    D. the leader assume a confident, positive approach

27. When starting a new craft program, it is IMPORTANT that the leader

    A. employ much technical vocabulary unfamiliar to most members of the group in order to establish his expert status
    B. exclude from the group anyone whose skill in the craft is superior to the leader so as to prevent dual leadership
    C. start with material familiar to most members of the group so as to build confidence in their ability to absorb what is to come
    D. treat the group as homogeneous, disregarding individual differences

28. The one of the following which BEST expresses a desirable characteristic of group leadership is:

    A. Advises the group as to suitable objectives and means of accomplishing them; assists in settling disagreements arising within the group
    B. Arranges effective intercommunication among the group; does not permit any conflicts to arise
    C. Permits the members of the group to set its own objectives and the means of accomplishing them; does not intercede to resolve conflicts
    D. Sets proper objectives of the group and instructs in the correct method of accomplishing those objectives; settles any disputes that may arise

28.___

Questions 29-43.

DIRECTIONS: Column I lists a series of activities numbered from 29 through 43, each of which is to be matched with one of the choices given in Column II. For each item of Column I, write in the space at the right the letter in front of the choice in Column II with which it is MOST closely related.

COLUMN I

29. Bait casting
30. Block printing
31. Circle game
32. Dramatics
33. Finger painting
34. Folk song
35. Handicraft with cloth
36. Leather craft
37. Nature study
38. Net game
39. Pottery craft
40. Relay game
41. Square dance
42. Woodworking
43. Word game

COLUMN II

A. Allemande
B. Awl
C. Batik
D. Blue-tail Fly
E. Egg balancing
F. Ghost
G. Kiln
H. Linoleum
I. Loop Tennis
J. Miming
K. Miter box
L. Mumblety-peg
M. Newcomb
N. Over and Under
O. Puck
P. Skishing
Q. Soap flakes and starch
R. Terrarium
S. Three Deep
T. Titanium
U. Wicket

29.___
30.___
31.___
32.___
33.___
34.___
35.___
36.___
37.___
38.___
39.___
40.___
41.___
42.___
43.___

44. In dealing with an individual who displays his insecurity by aggressive behavior, the group leader should FIRST

    A. directly champion the individual to the group
    B. indicate acceptance of the individual by the leader
    C. insist that the individual withdraw from the group for a temporary period
    D. permit the group to attempt to deal with the individual

45. Studies of clubs and gangs have indicated certain basic facts about them.
    The one of the following which is NOT a basic characteristic of clubs or gangs is:

    A. Participation in either street gangs or street clubs is a part of the growing up process of some adolescents
    B. Repressive measures in dealing with antisocial behavior of clubs or gangs brings about basic changes in attitudes and behavior
    C. Some clubs or gangs, as a result of fundamental factors such as poor housing, racial discrimination, or emotional maladjustment of their leaders or members, have developed patterns of antisocial behavior
    D. To be effective in modifying antisocial behavior of clubs or gangs, it is imperative that a social worker be assigned to only one street club or gang

46. A basketball team in a community center was composed of a group of boys who were inseparable in most of their free time. The group became involved in some antisocial activities because the most vocal and influential members of the group were able to persuade some of the other boys who individually would not have committed the wrong acts. This latter minority was PROBABLY involved because the

    A. community center had failed to break up the team so that the delinquent boys would not have had a chance to corrupt the non-delinquent
    B. community center had failed to sublimate the adolescent's need for adventure
    C. members of the group were inherently delinquentprone
    D. need to belong to the group was so great that some boys agreed to behavior which was actually unacceptable to them

47. Hostile feelings held by a few members of an organized group are LEAST likely to be reduced by

    A. appointing a committee to deal with the problem, with the disgruntled ones made members of the committee
    B. holding group discussions of the reasons for the hostility
    C. insisting upon the will of the majority
    D. making concessions to the hostile group

48. Of the following statements concerning groups, it is MOST correct to say:

    A. Hostile feelings are wrong and must be weeded out
    B. Signs of hostility prove the group was poorly chosen
    C. So long as hostile feelings are felt with equal strength by every member of a group, the group will function efficiently together
    D. The need to be together subordinates hostile feelings

49. The one of the following agencies which has initial jurisdiction over children apprehended by the Police Department is the

   A. City Youth Board
   B. Family Court
   C. Juvenile Aid Bureau
   D. Youth Bureau

50. The one of the following which BEST characterizes the philosophy of the City Youth Board is:

   A. Reform the gang; efforts to improve individuals as such have proved fruitless
   B. Search for the child in need; do not wait for the child to express a willingness to accept help
   C. Work through the children; the children will reform the parents
   D. Work through the parents; they will teach their children what is right

KEY (CORRECT ANSWERS)

1. C	11. B	21. C	31. S	41. A
2. C	12. A	22. C	32. J	42. K
3. C	13. C	23. A	33. Q	43. F
4. B	14. D	24. C	34. D	44. B
5. D	15. C	25. B	35. C	45. B
6. B	16. B	26. B	36. B	46. D
7. B	17. A	27. C	37. R	47. C
8. B	18. B	28. A	38. M	48. D
9. C	19. A	29. P	39. G	49. C
10. C	20. B	30. H	40. N	50. B

TEST 2

DIRECTIONS: Each question or incomplete statement is followed by several suggested answers or completions. Select the one that BEST answers the question or completes the statement. *PRINT THE LETTER OF THE CORRECT ANSWER IN THE SPACE AT THE RIGHT.*

1. The GREATEST value to the playground program in having an effective public relations program is that it

   A. creates public appreciation of the professional nature of recreation work
   B. encourages participation
   C. helps to interpret the program and solicit support for it
   D. is the most effective means of assuring administrative approval of a satisfactory budget

   1.____

2. In handling publicity for a recreation program, it is BEST to

   A. allow public demand to govern the rate at which information is given them
   B. coordinate all publicity with special outstanding recreational events
   C. intensify publicity efforts whenever the public loses interest
   D. maintain constant flow of information to the public at all times

   2.____

3. Of the following, the MOST important reason for the professional staff in a community center to keep detailed records of an organized group is the contribution the record makes toward

   A. better understanding of individuals and the group as a whole
   B. effective program planning for the entire center
   C. proper selection of participants for tournaments or festivals
   D. interpreting the services of the program to the public

   3.____

4. Of the following, the MOST important reason for part-time workers in a community center to keep detailed records of organized groups is the contribution the record makes toward

   A. interpreting the services of the program to the public
   B. effective program planning for the entire center
   C. proper selection of participants for tournaments or festivals
   D. providing continuity of information in the event that group leadership changes

   4.____

5. The GENERAL purposes for which staff meetings of recreation personnel should be called are share experiences and problems,

   A. reprimand the inefficient, prepare plans, and coordinate effort
   B. evaluate activities and services, explain new sports and activities, and coordinate effort
   C. evaluate activities and services, prepare plans, and coordinate effort
   D. evaluate activities and services, prepare plans, and introduce new members of the staff

   5.____

6. In planning the conduct of a staff meeting to be called for the purpose of solving a particular problem, the one of the following which should occur after all the others is the

   A. adoption of a plan of action
   B. definite allocation of responsibility
   C. discussion of the problem by the supervisor
   D. exchange of opinions

7. At a staff conference, one member of the staff frequently has good ideas but he expresses them poorly.
It would be BEST for the supervisor to

   A. disregard the manner in which the ideas are presented
   B. permit the staff member to express his ideas and for the supervisor to rephrase the ideas presented in a more readily understandable manner
   C. postpone consideration of these ideas to the next conference so that the staff member can put his ideas in clearer and better form
   D. suggest that the staff member explain his ideas to the supervisor before the staff meeting so that the supervisor may present the ideas at the meeting in a more readily understandable manner

8. The method of allowing news of forthcoming changes in policy to be spread by rumor and other unofficial means is

   A. *bad*, because it detracts from the status of the lower level supervisors
   B. *bad*, because newly appointed employees will not get the necessary information
   C. *good*, because it permits changes to be made in the policy before its official announcement in response to valid objections which may be expressed
   D. *good*, because it results in the most rapid dissemination of information about the new policy

9. Prestige is a factor which, consciously or unconsciously, is considered by most supervisors to be important.
From the point of view of good management, enhancing the prestige of a supervisor is

   A. *bad*, because it builds up the supervisor's importance without equally achieving the aims of management
   B. *good*, as a measure of economy since it may serve as a substitute for increased salary
   C. *good*, because it increases the supervisor's identification with, and support of, management aims
   D. *good*, in order to build the subordinates' awareness of, and belief in, the supervisor's authority

10. A desirable characteristic of a good supervisor is that he should

    A. identify himself with his subordinates rather than with higher management
    B. inform subordinates of forthcoming changes in policies and programs only when they directly affect the subordinates' activities
    C. make advancement of the subordinates contingent on personal loyalty to the supervisor
    D. make promises to subordinates only when sure of the ability to keep them

11. The supervisor who is MOST likely to be successful is the one who

    A. refrains from exercising the special privileges of his position
    B. maintains a formal attitude toward his subordinates
    C. maintains an informal attitude toward his subordinates
    D. represents the desires of his subordinates to his superiors

12. Application of sound principles of human relations by a supervisor may be expected to _____ the need for formal discipline.

    A. decrease
    B. have no effect on
    C. increase
    D. obviate

13. The MOST important generally approved way to maintain or develop high morale in one's subordinates is to

    A. give warnings and reprimands in a jocular manner
    B. excuse from staff conferences those employees who are busy
    C. keep them informed of new developments and policies of higher management
    D. refrain from criticizing their faults directly

14. In training subordinates, an important principle for the supervisor to recognize is that

    A. a particular method of instruction will be of substantially equal value for all employees in a given title
    B. it is difficult to train people over 50 years of age because they have little capacity for learning
    C. persons undergoing the same course of training will learn at different rates of speed
    D. training can seldom achieve its purpose unless individual instruction is the chief method used

15. Over an extended period of time, a subordinate is MOST likely to become and remain most productive if the supervisor

    A. accords praise to the subordinate whenever his work is satisfactory, withholding criticism except in the case of very inferior work
    B. avoids both praise and criticism except for outstandingly good or bad work performed by the subordinate
    C. informs the subordinate of his shortcomings, as viewed by management, while according praise only when highly deserved
    D. keeps the subordinate informed of the degree of satisfaction with which his performance of the job is viewed by management

16. A playground director has not properly carried out the orders of his assistant supervisor of recreation on several occasions to the point where he has been successively warned, reprimanded, and severely reprimanded. When the playground director once again does not carry out orders, the PROPER action for the assistant supervisor of recreation to take is to

    A. bring the playground director up on charges of failing to perform his duties properly
    B. have a serious discussion with the playground director explaining the need for the orders and the necessity for carrying them out

C. recommend that the playground director be transferred to another district
D. severely reprimand the playground director again, making clear that no further deviation will be countenanced

17. A supervisor with several subordinates becomes aware that two of these subordinates are neither friendly nor congenial.
In making assignments, it would be BEST for the supervisor to

    A. disregard the situation
    B. disregard the situation in making a choice of assignment but emphasize the need for teamwork
    C. investigate the situation to find out who is at fault, and give that individual the less desirable assignments until such time as he corrects his attitude
    D. place the unfriendly subordinates in positions where they have as little contact with one another as possible

18. A group of newly appointed recreation leaders have been assigned to your jurisdiction.
Of the following, the MOST important thing for you to do when they report for work on their first day is to

    A. assign them to definite areas of responsibility
    B. describe to them sickness, absence, and vacation policies
    C. discuss with them the social philosophy of public recreation
    D. inform them of the general character and duties of the job

19. Assume that a new procedure in the conduct of tournaments has been adopted which you, as supervisor, think may meet with staff resistance.
To accomplish the general aims of supervision and to minimize any anticipated resistance to the new procedure, it would be BEST to

    A. approach the members of the staff individually and, on a personal basis, gain their promise of cooperation
    B. explain the reason for the new procedure at a staff meeting and advise the staff that they must accept it regardless of their personal feelings
    C. elect or appoint a staff committee to study and report on the advantages and disadvantages of the new procedure
    D. issue detailed instructions on the use of the new procedure to facilitate its application

20. When you become aware that a recreation leader under your supervision has failed to follow the proper procedure in certain cases and has concealed the fact that he has failed to do so, it would be BEST for you to

    A. discuss with him both the error and the reason for its concealment, with the aim of improving the relationship between superior and subordinate
    B. explain the proper procedure to him and reprimand him for having concealed his failure to follow it
    C. make no mention of the matter but supervise him more closely in the future
    D. tell him that the proper procedure must be followed since failure to do so is a violation of the rules of the department

21. One of the basic objectives of recreation is satisfaction or enjoyment. 21.____
    The one of the following which contributes LEAST to the accomplishment of this objective is

    A. being accepted and wanted by others of the same age
    B. complete escape through an interesting and all-consuming activity
    C. recognition from others by applause or praise
    D. receiving material recognition for effort

22. In discussing public schools and public recreation centers, recreation leaders have 22.____
    agreed that

    A. education is not an important aim of public recreation
    B. in both areas, education for the worthy use of leisure is essential
    C. motivation for learning is greater in public schools than in recreation centers
    D. the methods of teaching are the same in the two areas

23. The one of the following which the recreation leader is LEAST expected to develop in 23.____
    children participating in a playground program is

    A. acceptance of the rules of the game or activity
    B. cooperation with other children
    C. respect for the equipment being used
    D. skill in the activity

24. Using the family, rather than the individual, as the central unit in the development of a 24.____
    public recreation program is

    A. *desirable* but expensive to operate
    B. *undesirable* and expensive to operate
    C. *desirable* because it is inexpensive to operate
    D. *undesirable* except for the saving in operating expenses

25. In thinking of juvenile delinquency prevention, the MOST limited and narrow approach to 25.____
    prevention would stress

    A. improving all aspects of life that affect children's social, moral, religious, educational, and physical growth
    B. promoting healthy personality development of all children
    C. reducing recidivism should take priority over reaching children not yet law violators
    D. reaching that segment which predictive signs indicate are the potential delinquents

26. In starting a recreational program for people over sixty-five years of age, it is of FIRST 26.____
    importance to provide

    A. arts and crafts equipment and supplies
    B. a sense of belonging
    C. leadership and remove taxing responsibility
    D. very comfortable surroundings

27. In preparing a program of games, physical strength and stamina of the expected partici- 27.___
pants must be considered. When preparing a program for a group of 10-year-olds, it
should be remembered that the girls of this age are

   A. as strong and active as boys of the same age
   B. more physically mature than boys of the same age
   C. passing through a period of physical weakness
   D. weaker and have less stamina than boys of the same age in all probability

28. In conducting a party for children in the eight to twelve year age group, it is LEAST impor- 28.___
tant that

   A. children understand that controls on wild behavior exist
   B. instructions for games be brief and entertaining
   C. the games involve all of the children at once
   D. there be several games in which girls and boys form partnerships

29. The MOST desirable means of attracting children under ten years of age to the recre- 29.___
ation center is to conduct a special event such as a

   A. costume parade   B. field day
   C. marbles tournament   D. song contest

30. In laying out a playground to serve a highly populated urban area, it is BEST to 30.___

   A. eliminate landscaping and arrangements that consume space
   B. make use of all available space even at the expense of not grouping activity areas
      by age level or degree of required supervision
   C. provide for multiple use of many play areas
   D. revise standard dimensions of sports diamonds and courts to enable the inclusion
      of an unusually large variety of activities

31. Of the following, the MOST important consideration in planning a playground site for chil- 31.___
dren 4 to 6 years of age is

   A. confining fence or hedge
   B. grassy area
   C. hard surface area (such as asphalt)
   D. plenty of shade

32. Registration of participants as a tool for evaluating the effectiveness of a recreation pro- 32.___
gram is

   A. a procedure receiving increasing acceptance for use with all activities
   B. generally too cumbersome a procedure to be of any value
   C. of value only when no attendance counts are made
   D. practical for use with many activities but impractical for use with many other activi-
      ties

33. Special events are considered a desirable aspect of any playground program CHIEFLY 33.___
because they

   A. add variety and a change of pace to the program
   B. are incentives to participants

C. are one of the best ways to terminate a seasonal program
D. have tremendous public relations value

34. One of the basic reasons why it is important for group leaders to focus on individual and group objectives is that doing so

    A. guarantees a better planned schedule of activities
    B. insures a fairer process in program planning
    C. reduces the likelihood that the group's individual needs will be the basis for program planning
    D. reduces the likelihood that the leader's own individual needs will be the basis on which the groups' program is determined

34._____

35. Recreation changes in character and emphasis from one age group to another.
It is MOST characteristic of the pre-school child as compared with older children that the pre-school child

    A. likes to play with others
    B. likes vigorous games
    C. plays very much by himself
    D. possesses a group spirit

35._____

36. When members of two racial groups participate in common social and recreational activities, the MOST likely effect on racial prejudice is to

    A. increase the prejudice
    B. decrease the prejudice
    C. either increase it or decrease it, depending upon the effective leadership of the groups
    D. have no effect upon the prejudice

36._____

37. Among the regular users of a community recreation center are two well-defined groups, organized on a racial basis, which have little or no contact with each other.
An attempt to dispel the existing racial prejudice may BEST be made by organizing a center-wide

    A. dance requiring cooperative action by both groups for planning and preparations
    B. party requiring cooperative action by both groups for planning and preparation
    C. dance to be sponsored and conducted by one group and to which the other group will be invited
    D. party to be sponsored and conducted by one group and to which the other group will be invited

37._____

38. The one of the following which is NOT a basic principle governing the successful operation of a teen center is:

    A. The closing time should not be too late, about 10 P.M.
    B. Separate problems should be set up for the young teenagers and for the older teenagers
    C. The center should be open whenever it will be patronized by a sizable group of teenagers
    D. The center should remain open during school holidays and vacation times

38._____

39. When a newly appointed recreation leader requests advice from an assistant supervisor of recreation on the proper way to handle several disruptive but not disturbed children who frequent the playground to which he has been assigned, the assistant supervisor of recreation should suggest that the recreation leader

    A. exclude the children from the playground since they are a disruptive influence
    B. include the children in activities and accord them special recognition
    C. make his own decisions since he knows the children best
    D. refer the children to a psychiatric clinic for help in achieving proper social adjustment

40. By a majority vote, after full discussion and participation, the members of a teenage canteen agreed upon a set of regulations. A minority threatened to withdraw from the canteen if the rules were enforced.
    The principle to be recognized in this situation is:

    A. The rules probably were too stringent and should be revised so that the minority will have its rights preserved
    B. The basic aims of democracy are not violated if we insist upon conformity once the rules have been agreed upon
    C. The basic aims of democracy are violated if we insist upon conformity once the rules have been agreed upon
    D. The basic aims of democracy require that this decision be vetoed in the interests of the minority

41. A community center program for teenagers has been criticized because the participants do not get home until several hours after the center closed.
    In such a situation, it is BEST that the center director

    A. advise the parents that he can do nothing about the time their children arrive home because he has no control over the children after they leave the center
    B. confer with the parents and with the teenagers to establish a home arrival time acceptable to community mores
    C. extend the closing time of the center to conform with the hour that the teenagers usually get home
    D. warn the teenagers that the program will be discontinued unless they go home within a short time after the closing of the center

42. It is of importance for a teen center to use a substantial part of its funds to arouse and maintain interest among a high proportion of its potential and active members.
    This objective is MOST likely to be accomplished by

    A. arranging for sweaters, pins, or other emblems with the name of the center emblazoned on it to be distributed to all members at a nominal charge
    B. careful planning to provide a wide range of activities
    C. operating on a *come and go* basis
    D. restricting the program to providing a meeting and lounging place, conducting dances, sponsoring parties, and providing opportunities for certain games

43. The organization of neighborhood recreation councils or committees should be encouraged by an assistant supervisor of recreation CHIEFLY because such councils or committees can

    A. help plan the recreation program and promote public interest in it in the neighborhood
    B. help train volunteer leaders
    C. sponsor tournaments and pageants
    D. supervise and evaluate the existing recreation programs in terms of community needs

44. The MOST valid means of evaluating the effectiveness of a program of recreation or informal education is

    A. appraisal of community support for the program as evidenced by Community Chest support (for private agencies) or tax support (for public services)
    B. appraisal of the program's purposes and performance in the light of community-wide conditions, needs, and services
    C. documented testimony of its value given by those who have participated in the program
    D. participation in the program by a substantial majority of the community

45. The author of A PHILOSOPHY OF RECREATION AND LEISURE is

    A. Bancroft   B. Butler   C. Meyer   D. Nash

46. An assistant supervisor of recreation should recognize that the training of recreation leaders is

    A. never complete, and they require continual additional training and instruction
    B. seldom complete until they have received practical on-the-job training
    C. substantially complete once they have been broken in on the job, except for the need for occasional refresher courses
    D. substantially complete at the time they are appointed since they are professional trained people

47. If a supervisor realizes that he has mistakenly blamed one of his subordinates for a certain situation, it would be BEST for the supervisor to

    A. apologize to the subordinate at the next staff meeting
    B. apologize to the subordinate at the first opportunity
    C. ignore the occurrence
    D. make no mention of the mistake but act more favorably toward the subordinate as an indication that he has realized his error

48. If a subordinate requests a transfer to a job in another division, a job of no greater apparent value to the department and no greater value to the subordinate, it would be BEST for the supervisor to

    A. recommend the transfer only if the employee can give a good reason for wanting it
    B. refer the matter to his superior without recommendation

C. refuse the transfer on the grounds that it is not in the best interest of the department
D. request the employee to explain why he wants the transfer before recommending it

49. In teaching a new job to an employee, the MOST frequent of the following sources of difficulty is the

    A. desire of the employee to do the job in his own way
    B. incompatibility of personalities of teacher and pupil
    C. lack of confidence of the employee in his ability to learn
    D. unwillingness of the employee to learn something new

50. At a staff meeting of your division, you intend to present a new plan which you have devised.
    It is MOST important for you to

    A. anticipate objections and be prepared to answer them
    B. be able to demonstrate clearly the value of the plan in your own particular area of responsibility
    C. be prepared to scrap the plan if you encounter strong opposition
    D. prepare the plan so that it will probably be accepted without alteration

KEY (CORRECT ANSWERS)

1. C	11. D	21. D	31. A	41. B
2. D	12. A	22. B	32. D	42. B
3. A	13. C	23. C	33. B	43. A
4. D	14. C	24. A	34. D	44. B
5. C	15. D	25. C	35. C	45. D
6. B	16. A	26. B	36. C	46. A
7. B	17. D	27. A	37. B	47. B
8. A	18. D	28. D	38. A	48. D
9. D	19. B	29. A	39. B	49. C
10. D	20. A	30. C	40. B	50. A

EXAMINATION SECTION
TEST 1

DIRECTIONS: Each question or incomplete statement is followed by several suggested answers or completions. Select the one that BEST answers the question or completes the statement. *PRINT THE LETTER OF THE CORRECT ANSWER IN THE SPACE AT THE RIGHT.*

1. A *typical* definition of recreation agreed upon by MOST authorities would be
    A. voluntarily chosen leisure activities, for pleasure or personal benefit, meeting community standards and needs
    B. pleasurable activities provided by community agencies without social purpose
    C. whatever people want to do, because they want to do it
    D. purposeful activities, such as anti-delinquency, addiction treatment, or golden age programs, which make use of trips and cultural activities

1.____

2. In the past, it was argued that recreation programs for youth prevented juvenile delinquency.
Today the majority of social work or recreation authorities would MOST probably support the view that
    A. recreation is the key element in any anti-delinquency program
    B. recreation has proved to be of little value in anti-delinquency programs
    C. juvenile delinquents usually are anti-social and disruptive and should be kept out of organized recreation programs
    D. juvenile delinquency treatment requires varied services, including education, job training, recreation, and improved housing

2.____

3. The MAJOR professional organization serving the recreation field in the United States today is the
    A. American Institute of Park and Recreation Practitioners
    B. National Recreation and Park Association
    C. National Recreation Association
    D. American Association for Health, Physical Education, and Recreation

3.____

4. Varied theories of play have been developed by psychologists, philosophers, and others.
One TRADITIONAL theory that sees play as the means through which children prepare for the demands of adult life is the _____ theory.
    A. instinct-practice   B. catharsis
    C. recapitulation   D. relaxation

4.____

5. Which of the following statements BEST supports the self-expression theory of play as developed by Mason and Mitchell?
    A. Activities are engaged in for the purpose of overcoming natural human inertness.

5.____

B. Due to the pressures for self-maintenance and other compulsions, human beings use play as outlets for frustration.
C. Human physiological and anatomical structure are independent of any specific form of play.
D. Because human beings are dynamic animals, activity is a primary need of life.

6. Of the following, the MOST recent psychological theory of play is the
   A. pleasure principle theory (Freud)
   B. play extraversion theory (Piaget)
   C. arousal or stimulation theory (Berlynne)
   D. aggressive-release theory (Schiller-Spencer-Groos)

7. Generally, the BASIC philosophy of public recreation departments today is to
   A. serve all groups as fully as possible
   B. place the greatest emphasis on helping the poor
   C. serve primarily the middle and upper classes
   D. concentrate on children and youth

8. The one of the following which is NOT a widely accepted goal of public recreation departments is to
   A. provide constructive and creative outlets for leisure
   B. meet participants' physical, mental, social, and creative needs
   C. develop large numbers of athletes to play on college or pro teams
   D. strengthen family life and help community unity

9. The growth of the organized recreation movement in the United States was promoted by several social factors.
   Of the following, the one which did NOT contribute to such growth is
   A. the increase in leisure through the shortened work-week, more holidays, and longer vacations
   B. the development of movies, television, and radio as major forms of entertainment
   C. the general affluence and mobility in society
   D. more liberal attitudes toward leisure on the part of religious, educational, and government authorities

10. Recognition by state certifying boards or departments is one of the formal methods through which professionals in fields such as law or medicine are approved.
    Today, certification for recreation professionals exists in
    A. a small number of states   B. all fifty states
    C. no states   D. about half the states

11. Supervisors should be able to advise recently appointed recreation workers on the appropriate selection of activities for specific age groups.
    When planning for after-school recreation activities for boys of elementary-school age, the MOST useful type of game would usually be

A. low-organized games, such as dodge-ball, kick-ball, and relays
B. table games, such as parcheessi, backgammon, and chess
C. encounter games and touching games, like those used in sensitivity groups
D. mental games and contests, such as ghost, coffee-pot, and twenty questions

12. Since anti-social youth are often unwilling to enter highly structured activities and programs, or may be barred from recreation centers, they are frequently not served by community recreation agencies.
Of the following, the BEST way to serve such youth is to
    A. develop entirely new kinds of activities that will appeal to delinquents because of their thrill-seeking nature
    B. organize special community center programs to serve only delinquent youth who have been in trouble with the law
    C. assign roving or street gang workers to make contact with unaffiliated youth and gangs to involve them in constructive activities
    D. wait until they are sent to correctional institutions and then give them concentrated recreation programs there

12._____

13. Adolescent girls in youth houses (detention or remand centers) often have poor self-concepts.
Of the following, the TYPICAL approach used by recreation workers in such settings to help these girls improve their self-concepts is to
    A. tell such girls at appropriate times that they are just as good as anybody
    B. organize self-improvement classes to teach skills in make-up, dressing, or modeling
    C. sponsor sports teams, such as basketball or volleyball, which can compete with other institutions
    D. administer personality tests to diagnose their problems

13._____

14. Many teenage boys are fascinated by automobiles.
Of the following, a USEFUL way for a creation worker to deal with this interest would be to
    A. sponsor drag-racing meets in a conveniently located park or raceway
    B. develop an automotive hobby car repair club in a community center or nearby garage
    C. arrange a contest to select one boy to go on a trip to the Indianapolis 500 to watch the big race
    D. develop a joint program with a school bus company to train boys as junior bus operators

14._____

15. According to the traditional *space standards* employed for the past several decades to measure the need for open space and recreation facilities in American communities, there should be AT LEAST
    A. one neighborhood playground for each 1,500 children under age 12
    B. three acres of outdoor recreation space for each 1,000 residents
    C. one acre of outdoor recreation space for each 100 residents
    D. one community center for each 5,000 children and teenagers

15._____

16. *Therapeutic recreation service* is the term applied today to programs which serve the physically, mentally, or socially handicapped.
    For BEST results, such programs should be provided in
    A. institutions such as mental hospitals or schools for the mentally handicapped
    B. community settings such as after-care centers or community programs for the physically disabled
    C. both institutional and community settings
    D. private or voluntary facilities

16.____

17. Social group work is BEST defined as a method of social work which
    A. assigns people to groups for intensive psychotherapy as a means of crisis intervention
    B. helps people improve their social functioning and ability to cope with interpersonal problems
    C. utilizes unskilled community people to take over many social work organizations
    D. relies on the leader's ability to mobilize people into effective instruments for community reform

17.____

18. Some recreation departments operate multi-service senior centers which provide social services related to nutrition, health needs, legal, or housing assistance, as well as recreation.
    This type of program is regarded by leading authorities in the field of recreation as
    A. usually not the function of a recreation department since it has proved to be a hindrance to customary social and recreational programs
    B. clearly not the function of a recreation department and should be discontinued
    C. an appropriate function of a recreation department and is justified by Federal funding guidelines in this field
    D. an appropriate function of a recreation department only when the program is receiving a grant from the State Department of Aging

18.____

19. The view that MOST social workers generally have of recreation is that it is
    A. almost identical to social work
    B. a competitor with social work for public funds
    C. a medium through which they can involve and work constructively with participants
    D. strictly for fun, without a serious purpose

19.____

20. The three MAJOR areas of social work training and practice are
    A. group work, psychiatric case work, and neighborhood management
    B. community analysis, case work, and agency supervision
    C. group rehabilitation, psychiatric community development, and case work
    D. case work, group work, and community organization

20.____

5 (#1)

21. Which of the following BEST expresses the program objectives of recreation programs provided by the municipal agencies as a whole?
They should
   A. emphasize after-school and summer vacation play programs
   B. provide activities for various age groups
   C. concentrate on programs for younger boys and teenage youth
   D. meet social needs that are unsatisfied by family relationships

21.____

22. Of the following, which is the LEAST appropriate basis for choosing the recreation program activities for a community center, hospital, or other institutions? The
   A. needs and interests of the participants based on their age, sex, socio-economic background, etc.
   B. overall philosophy and goals of the sponsoring agency
   C. ability of the agency to offer certain activities based on its staff resources, facilities, funding, etc.
   D. degree to which prospective participants are personally acquainted with one another

22.____

23. The MOST common approach to developing schedules of program activities in municipal recreation departments is to organize them
   A. on a centralized basis, that is, each central office or county headquarters develops a precise schedule that must be followed in each center or playground
   B. on a *report* system, that is, each center or playground develops its individual schedule and must report daily on which activities were carried out, and which were not
   C. on the basis of seasonal interests, with different schedules being developed for summer, fall, winter, and spring
   D. according to whatever seems to be of interest on a particular day, emphasizing flexibility

23.____

24. A difficult problem in scheduling recreation programs is to have personnel available at needed times.
The BEST approach for dealing with this problem is to
   A. change recreation leadership jobs to the four-day workweek that has become so popular in industry
   B. make leadership assignment schedules more flexible to insure coverage for special events, including evening and weekend activities
   C. assign all personnel a noon-to-8 P.M. daily schedule
   D. convert all full-time leadership jobs into part-time per session positions and then assign these as needed

24.____

25. Ideally, the BEST program schedule for a community recreation center would be one which covers
   A. the full day and evening to permit scheduling for senior citizens, housewives, or pre-schoolers, as well as youth and other adults
   B. from 3:00 P.M. to 10:00 P.M. since this is the time when children and youth are out of school

25.____

33

C. the daily hours of maximum use, based on participant demand, because of the financial limitations of many centers
D. daytime hours only since most people today will not come out at night because of fear of crime

KEY (CORRECT ANSWERS)

1.	A		11.	A
2.	D		12.	C
3.	B		13.	B
4.	A		14.	B
5.	D		15.	C
6.	C		16.	C
7.	A		17.	B
8.	C		18.	C
9.	B		19.	C
10.	A		20.	D

21. B
22. D
23. C
24. B
25. A

TEST 2

DIRECTIONS: Each question or incomplete statement is followed by several suggested answers or completions. Select the one that BEST answers the question or completes the statement. *PRINT THE LETTER OF THE CORRECT ANSWER IN THE SPACE AT THE RIGHT.*

1. Active team games during the summer months of July and August at a neighborhood playground are BEST scheduled for 1.____
   A. early afternoon and late evening
   B. Saturday only (morning and afternoon)
   C. morning, late afternoon, and evening
   D. evening only (after 7:30 P.M.

2. Various activities help to keep attendance at a summer playground high by building interest and enthusiasm among participants. 2.____
   Which of the following is the POOREST example of such activities?
   A. Weekly special events, such as pet shows, bicycle rodeos, hobby fairs, etc.
   B. End-of-summer festivals, carnivals, play-days, exhibitions, etc., for which participants prepare for several weeks
   C. Trips using chartered or public transportation to state parks, swimming pools, etc. for those attending regularly
   D. Daily tutoring programs of remedial education for those who are having difficulty in school

3. Of the various types of activities sponsored by public recreation departments, the MOST popular single category, according to national surveys, is 3.____
   A. services for the handicapped (such as the mentally handicapped, blind, or physical disabled)
   B. the performing arts (music, drama, and dance)
   C. social activities (clubs, parties, dances, etc.)
   D. sports of all kinds (such as baseball, football, and basketball)

4. The MOST typical method of organizing youth sports leagues in public recreation departments is to 4.____
   A. encourage recreation leaders to organize and coach several teams themselves, running their own tournaments
   B. reduce competitive play, which is harmful to youth, and concentrate instead on cooperative games
   C. work with community organizations that set up and coach their own teams
   D. have children on each block form their own teams and do their own coaching

5. Each craft activity has a specific set of items describing its equipment or process. The following words, *bisque, greenware,* and *slab-construction,* are used in reference to 5.____
   A. ceramics   B. metalcrafts
   C. glass-blowing   D. decoupage

6. According to their degree of difficulty, various arts and crafts activities are usually suited to different age levels,
   Which of the following would be MOST suited to pre-school children?
   A. Macrame
   B. Watercolor painting
   C. Fingerpainting
   D. Jewelry-making

7. Among the most popular recreational sport activities are basketball, baseball, and bowling.
   The terms which do NOT apply to any of these three games are
   A. strike, dribble, sacrifice
   B. linebacker, offside, foot-fault
   C. spare, infield, hoop
   D. walking, infield, alley

8. Which of the following activities would LEAST likely be found in a municipal recreation department's music program?
   A. Rock-and-roll band practice and competition
   B. Chamber music groups
   C. Drum and bugle corps
   D. Informal community singing or folk music activities

9. Informal dramatics activities are often used with children and teenagers.
   Which of the following would be MOST likely to promote creative dramatic skills and interest among beginners?
   A. One-act play contests with scripts, costumes, and scenery
   B. Choral reading of popular poetry
   C. Memorizing and reciting sections from famous Broadway plays
   D. Improvisational dramatic games, like prop or paper bag plays

10. In the past, many recreation departments sponsored holiday festivals or special events such as the English May Day Festival.
    Today, the trend is to
    A. have such festivals reflect ethnic group interests such as Black Culture or Hispanic-American Arts
    B. eliminate all such events since there is little interest in them
    C. deal mainly with historical commemorations since these would appeal to traditional patriotism
    D. make festivals *future-minded* by dealing with the Space Age or America of the Future

11. Of the following types of tournaments, the type which can be completed MOST quickly in individual sports such as fencing or table-tennis is the _____ tournament.
    A. round robin
    B. elimination
    C. challenge (pyramid)
    D. challenge (ladder)

12. Recreation has been affected by several key trends in psychiatric treatment.
    Which of the following is NOT such a key trend?
    A. Reducing patient populations in large, distant state institutions and setting up local mental health facilities, with after-care or day-clinic programs

B. Reliance on chemotherapy, which makes patients more receptive to programs
C. The development of activity therapy programs in many hospitals, which include education, recreation, occupational therapy, and similar activities
D. Hiring of psychiatric patients as recreation aides, which may lead to employment after discharge

13. In recreation programs serving the seriously physically handicapped, such as those who have suffered strokes, amputations, etc., the PRIMARY program objective is to
    A. help patients develop potential skills using the facilities of community and out-of-hospital recreational programs
    B. raise funds, through parties, bazaars, special shows, etc., that patients put on to meet special patient needs
    C. use recreation as a specific treatment modality that will restore function, help patients learn to use prosthesis, etc.
    D. make patients accept their limitations and the fact that they cannot participate in many normal recreation activities

13.____

14. The majority of mentally handicapped teenagers or young adults live in the community, rather than in institutions. Recreation for such persons has several important goals.
    Of the following, the LEAST appropriate recreation goal for such persons is to
    A. help them improve the poor coordination and overcome the obesity typical of many such persons through physical activity
    B. help them acquire social skills and improve behavior and appearance so they will be able to mingle with others more effectively
    C. provide enjoyable and socially desirable leisure activities in order to make life more satisfying
    D. improve their I.Q.'s in order to help them get better jobs or be able to continue in school

14.____

15. Senior centers that serve older persons should meet the important needs of these individuals.
    Of the following, it would be LEAST appropriate for such centers to meet the need for
    A. full-time employment by acting as a placement bureau for center members
    B. modified physical activity to help keep older people active and prevent physical deterioration
    C. social activity to help aging people make friends and avoid isolation
    D. program activities in which older people may do volunteer service in hospitals or in the community

15.____

16. In planning a recreation program at a low-income public housing project, it is important to establish an advisory board or council.
Such board or council should represent PRIMARILY the needs and interests of the
    A. civic groups
    B. residents
    C. parent-teacher associations
    D. youth workers

17. Public relations may have many objectives for a public recreation department. Of the following, the LEAST appropriate objective would be to
    A. provide accurate information about the department's overall program to the public at large
    B. encourage attendance and involvement at the department's events and regular programs
    C. build favorable public attitudes and encourage volunteer leadership in the programs
    D. encourage petitions or letter-writing campaigns for increased budgets for the department

18. The one of the following which is the MOST effective method for producing successful public relations is for recreation program administrators to
    A. appear before civil organizations
    B. satisfy users of programs
    C. publish effective brochures, announcements, and reports
    D. employ qualified, indigenous para-professionals

19. If a recreation supervisor were going to publicize a large one-day recreation event in his borough, the BEST way to promote attendance would be to
    A. use newspaper releases and distribute fliers to schools, churches, and temples
    B. place posters advertising the event in store windows
    C. put posters on playground bulletin boards
    D. make a filmstrip about the forthcoming event and distribute prints to civic groups

20. Assume that, as a recreation supervisor, you are directing a community center that has poor participation in programs by local residents.
Of the following, the MOST effective way for you to arouse more public interest would be to
    A. have the publicity office in your department's central office send out newspaper releases about the center
    B. form a neighborhood council to interpret the community's needs to you and help publicize your program
    C. frequent places where local people congregate
    D. plan a panel discussion in a nearby community auditorium to discuss the problem

5 (#2)

21. There are several possible approaches to getting community involvement in recreation service.
Of the following, the approach that would usually be LEAST workable would be to
    A. draw up a list of interested parents, clergymen, businessmen, local educators, etc., and invite them to a planning meeting about the neighborhood's recreation program
    B. announce an election to a recreation council, and select a slate of nominees, one for each square block so that local residents can elect their own representatives
    C. inquire as to whether the local Parent-Teachers Association will form a subcommittee interested in youth recreation to assist you
    D. work closely with the local district planning board to insure that they consider recreation as an important community service and to get their advice and help

21._____

22. Whether patients will be able to use their leisure constructively after discharge from the hospital is of vital concern to recreation workers in psychiatric hospitals.
Which of the following approaches would be LEAST useful in assuring continuing recreation service to a patient?
    A. Get a mimeographed list of recreation agencies in a patient's neighborhood and give him this before he is discharged
    B. Visit and talk with staff members of recreation agencies in a patient's neighborhood to make plans for their receiving the discharged patient
    C. Develop joint hospital-community recreation programs in special events, tours, entertainment programs, etc. to build a base of understanding for discharged patients
    D. Help the patient develop skills and interests in activities that will actually be available in his neighborhood after discharge

22._____

23. Therapeutic recreation seeks to help disabled persons enjoy a fuller, happier life. The question of whether they should be segregated in separate programs for the handicapped is an important one.
Which of the following statements about this group is MOST valid?
    A. The non handicapped in society are usually very sympathetic to the disabled and welcome them in all recreational and social programs.
    B. The handicapped are better off by themselves, in groups with others having similar disabilities, so they will not feel inferior.
    C. It is an important goal to integrate the handicapped with other persons whenever possible, although sometimes it may not be feasible.
    D. The handicapped should, without exception, be mixed with the non-handicapped in recreation programs.

23._____

24. Recreation is usually considered to be a positive force for improving social relations between different racial, ethnic, or socio-economic groups.
Of the following, which is the MOST valid statement about recreation and inter-group relations?

24._____

A. Public recreation is one field in which racial discrimination is not prohibited by law.
B. Recreation workers have an obligation to reflect and agree with the views of those they serve, regardless of the nature of such views.
C. Many of our community recreation programs are heavily racially segregated.
D. Prejudice is an inborn trait which often appears in competitive sports.

25. For minority-group youth, sports often provide upward social mobility into college and subsequent business careers.
However, of the following, a MAJOR problem that arises for such youth in their seeking upward social mobility is that
   A. unscrupulous college sports programs often exploit them
   B. they are unable to satisfactorily relate to members of their peer group
   C. sports fail to provide an outlet for hostility and aggression
   D. religious cults to which they become converted distract them from sports

KEY (CORRECT ANSWERS)

1.	C	11.	B
2.	D	12.	D
3.	D	13.	A
4.	C	14.	D
5.	A	15.	A
6.	C	16.	B
7.	B	17.	D
8.	B	18.	B
9.	D	19.	A
10.	A	20.	B

21.	B
22.	A
23.	C
24.	C
25.	A

TEST 3

DIRECTIONS: Each question or incomplete statement is followed by several suggested answers or completions. Select the one that BEST answers the question or completes the statement. *PRINT THE LETTER OF THE CORRECT ANSWER IN THE SPACE AT THE RIGHT.*

1. The trend in many recreation and park departments during the past several years has been toward providing special facilities and programs based on user fees and charges.
   The criticism MOST often made against such fees and charges is that
   A. few recreation directors have made serious efforts to serve residents of disadvantaged neighborhoods
   B. it increases the cost of servicing and maintaining facilities and services because standards must be raised
   C. public employees may be tempted to misappropriate funds or may be subject to accusations of dishonesty
   D. poor people may be unable to participate in what should be a publicly-available service

   1.____

2. With few exceptions, recreation directors have not been able to gain permission to operate programs regularly in school buildings.
   Of the following, the MOST successful way to improve this situation is to
   A. develop relationships and cooperative programs with local school board and district officials, or with individual school principals and custodians
   B. bring a class-action suit against the local schoolboard
   C. collect and submit legally valid petitions to the administration
   D. exert pressure on the schools by denying them use of parks or other recreational facilities for their physical education activities

   2.____

3. Many hospitals, particularly psychiatric hospitals, have therapists keep regular reports of patient participation in recreation programs.
   Of the following, the BEST use of such reports is to
   A. provide information which may be presented at meetings of the treatment team when the progress of patients is discussed
   B. provide a basis for a daily discussion between the patient and the therapist so the patient knows what is expected of him
   C. justify adverse actions such as denial of recreation privileges or the imposition of personal restrictions
   D. meet the requirements of mental hygiene laws as to standards of treatment and patient progress

   3.____

4. Much correspondence is likely to come into the central office of a public recreation department.
   Generally, all letters should be answered within one or two days UNLESS
   A. a letter is of a commonplace and unimportant nature
   B. the writer is unreasonably critical of the department
   C. form letters are used in place of personalized correspondence
   D. a letter requires special inquiries or decision-making

   4.____

41

5. One major type of report in recreation programs is based on the attendance of participants.
   Such report are GENERALLY considered to be
   A. an excellent quantitative and qualitative basis for evaluating the success of a program
   B. of primary use in operational research involving participant behavior and outcomes
   C. unnecessary since few departments continue to use attendance reports as a basis for funding
   D. quite inaccurate unless attendance counts are done systematically and staff members avoid inflating them

6. An informal survey of recreation in a hospital showed that patients who engaged regularly in the program were discharged from the hospital earlier than those who did not.
   Based on this information only, it would be MOST valid to say that
   A. such information has validity or meaning only to a qualified medical research person
   B. it is inconclusive whether there exists a cause and effect relationship between participation and discharge
   C. probably the healthier patients took part in the recreation program, and this was the reason for their earlier discharge
   D. recreation was the major determinant of earlier discharge

7. The one of the following it would be BEST to do when preparing or developing an annual report of a large recreational program is to
   A. gather material such as photos, program descriptions, news stories, and statistics which appeared during the courses of the year
   B. use narrative description rather than charts or graphs to present statistical data
   C. present only the positive aspects and successes of your program, elaborating when necessary to give a favorable picture
   D. give praise to key political figures in the report so they will support the program in the future

8. *Crash* programs of recreation have sometimes been rushed into slum areas as a response to the threat of violence. Often, the approach has been to present *portable* programs, for example, portable pools put into lots of streets, mobile libraries and nature displays, puppet shows, movies, and rock or soul music shows.
   Of the following, the MAJOR weakness of the *portable* recreation approach is that
   A. funds expended for such programs tend to be excessive and the general public is antagonized
   B. it emphasizes expending aimless energy rather than promoting social growth
   C. it meets only temporary recreation needs and fails to effect a permanent resolution of recreation problems

D. it tends to draw large numbers of youth out on the street, where they become riotous

9. A recent change in the concept of recreation as a public service is that it is now being thought of as a kind of social therapy.
   The MOST recent illustration of this has been the
   A. joint effort of religious agencies to develop new recreation programs, including year-round camping, for broken families
   B. expanded recreation programs in youth houses, remand institutions, and similar institutions run by the Department of Social Services
   C. new recreation program in private or multi-room occupancy hotels
   D. crash effort to provide recreation programs for alcoholics and older drug addicts

9.____

10. Low-income and racial minority youth tend to have very limited recreation interests. Often, teenage boys want to take part in basketball, but little else of an organized nature.
    For a recreation center director, what would be the BEST professional approach to this attitude?
    A. Begin with the interests they already have, then try to broaden their involvement in other recreation, athletic, or cultural activities
    B. Stick to basketball, their true interest, since they resist other activities
    C. Since they are able to play basketball in many neighborhood settings, eliminate this part of the program and offer new kinds of sports, cultural activities, and social events
    D. Rely on carefully prepared interest survey, and then offer youth only the activities and events they say they want

10.____

11. A NEW trend in many cities, with respect to the assignment of recreation leadership personnel, is to
    A. assign workers to one setting on a full-time, year-round basis so that they will be completely familiar with the work and do a superior job
    B. use seniority more than ever before, thereby giving the long-time employee freedom to pick his job
    C. rotate the assignments of workers from season-to-season or even day-to-day maximize output and improve morale by giving challenging assignments
    D. create new job shifts, such as one week from 9:00 to 5:00, next week from 2:00 to 10:00, etc.

11.____

12. Recreation counseling is becoming more widely used in many hospitals. Such counseling is PRIMARILY intended to
    A. help patients explore their leisure attitudes and interests and motivate them toward fuller participation after discharge
    B. teach patients a broad range of activities, such as sports, crafts, and social skills, that they can use after discharge
    C. use the recreation situation to uncover problems that can then be discussed when the patient gets therapeutic counseling

12.____

D. allow the patients to advise staff members on how best to organize the recreation program

13. A major problem today in many recreation and park departments is costly and destructive vandalism.
    Which of the following methods of dealing with this problem has NOT been widely accepted throughout the United States?
    A. Provide stronger enforcement of rules and better surveillance and protection of recreation and park facilities
    B. Offer more attractive programs since people are less likely to vandalize a facility if it is staffed and providing popular community activities
    C. Use new types of designs so that facilities are less prone to vandalism, such as windowless buildings, concrete benches and tables, etc.
    D. Abandon parks or playgrounds that have been repeatedly vandalized

13._____

14. The Board of Education has a strong commitment to recreation.
    Its recreation program focuses CHIEFLY on
    A. adult education programs in adult centers
    B. children and youth in after-school and evening centers
    C. the categories of pre-school, mentally handicapped, and senior citizens
    D. youth either considered to be pre-delinquent or adjudicated as delinquent

14._____

15. Those working to provide recreation to persons who have a physical, mental, emotional, or social disability frequently seek assistance from social service agencies.
    Which of the following pairs of agencies is LEAST likely to be helpful to them?
    A. Catholic Charities; Federation of Protestant Welfare Agencies
    B. United Cerebral Palsy of N.Y.C.; New York Association for the Blind
    C. New York Association for Retarded Children; National Wheelchair Athletic Association
    D. New York League for Crippled and Disabled Children, Adults and Aging; Handclasp for the Handicapped, Inc.

15._____

16. Throughout the nation, there has been an increase in senior centers for aging persons.
    Which of the following agencies does NOT sponsor special centers for aging persons?
    A. Housing Authority's low-income projects
    B. Office of Continuing Education
    C. Parks, Recreation and Cultural Affairs Administration
    D. Department of Social Services

16._____

17. The municipal department that has the PRIMARY responsibility for providing social services for youth, including recreation, is the
    A. Youth Activities Board
    B. Youth Services Agency
    C. United Block Association for Youth
    D. Bureau of Youth Community Services

17._____

18. If a recreation center director had severe problems with drug users in his neighborhood, the APPROPRIATE municipal department for him to ask for assistance is the
    A. Health and Hospitals Corporation
    B. Syanon or Phoenix House
    C. Department of Correction
    D. Addiction Services Agency

18.____

Questions 19-20.

DIRECTIONS: Questions 19 and 20 are to be answered SOLELY on the basis of the following passage.

This country was built on the puritanical belief that honest toil was the foundation of moral rectitude, the cement of society, and the uphill road to progress. Idleness was sin. As a result, we treat free time today as a conditional joy. We permit ourselves to relax only as a reward for hard work or as the recreation needed to put us back into shape for the job. Thus, the aimless delightful play of children gives way in adult life to a serious dedication to golf, the game that is so good for business.

19. According to the above passage, during former times in this country, respectable work was considered to be MOST NEARLY a
    A. way to improve health   B. form of recreation
    C. developer of good character D. reward for leisure

19.____

20. According to the point of view presented in the above passage, it would be MOST reasonable to assume that an employer would consider an employee's vacation to be a time for the employee to
    A. determine his own leisure time priorities
    B. loaf and relax
    C. learn new recreational skills
    D. increase his effectiveness at work

20.____

Questions 21-23.

DIRECTIONS: Questions 21 through 23 are to be answered SOLELY on the basis of the following passage.

One of the key supervisory problems in a large municipal recreation department is that many leaders are assigned to isolated playgrounds or small centers, where it is difficult to observe their work regularly. Often their facilities are extremely limited. In such settings, as well as in larger recreation centers, where many recreation leaders tend to have other jobs as well, there tends to be a low level of morale and incentive. Still, it is the supervisor's task to help recreation personnel to develop pride in their work, and to maintain a high level of performance. With isolated leaders, the supervisor may give advice or assistance. Leaders may be assigned to different tasks or settings during the year to maximize their productivity and provide new challenges. When it is clear that leaders are not willing to make a real effort to contribute to the department, the possibility of penalties must be considered, within the scope of departmental policy and the union contract. However, the supervisor should be constructive, encourage and assist workers to take a greater interest in their work, be innovative, and try to raise morale and to improve performance in positive ways.

21. The one of the following that would be the MOST appropriate title for the foregoing passage is
    A. SMALL COMMUNITY CENTERS – PRO AND CON
    B. PLANNING BETTER RECREATION PROGRAMS
    C. THE SUPERVISOR'S TASK IN UPGRADING PERSONNEL PERFORMANCE
    D. THE SUPERVISOR AND THE MUNICIPAL UNION – RIGHTS AND OBLIGATIONS

21.____

22. The above passage makes clear that recreation leadership performance in ALL recreation playgrounds and centers throughout a large city is
    A. generally above average, with good morale on the part of most recreation leaders
    B. beyond description since no one has ever observed or evaluated leaders
    C. a key test of the personnel department's effort to develop more effective hiring standards
    D. of mixed quality, with many recreation leaders having poor morale and a low level of achievement

22.____

23. According to the above passage, the supervisor's role is to
    A. use disciplinary action as his major tool in upgrading performance
    B. tolerate the lack of effort of individual employees since they are assigned to isolated playgrounds or small centers
    C. employ encouragement, advice, and, when appropriate, disciplinary action to improve performance
    D. inform the county supervisor whenever malfeasance or idleness is detected

23.____

Questions 24-25.

DIRECTIONS: Questions 24 and 25 are to be answered SOLELY on the basis of the following passage.

A recent study revealed some very concrete evidence concerning the relationship between avocations and mental health. A number of well-adjusted persons were surveyed as to the type, number, and duration of their hobbies. The findings were compared to those from a similar survey of mentally disturbed persons. In the well-adjusted group, both the number of hobbies and the intensity with which they were pursued were far greater than that of the mentally disturbed group.

24. According to the above passage, the study showed that
    A. well-adjusted people engage in hobbies more widely and deeply than do mentally disturbed people
    B. hobbies, if taken seriously, serve to keep most people mentally well

24.____

C. mental patients should be taught hobbies as a part of their therapy
D. the degree of interest in hobbies plays an important role in maintaining good mental health

25. In reference to the study mentioned in the above passage, it is MOST accurate to say that it appears to have 25._____
    A. been based on a carefully-structured, complex research design
    B. considered the variables of mental health and hobby involvement
    C. contained a general definition of mental health
    D. given evidence of a causal relationship between hobbies and mental health

---

KEY (CORRECT ANSWERS)

1.	D		11.	C
2.	A		12.	A
3.	A		13.	D
4.	D		14.	B
5.	D		15.	D
6.	B		16.	B
7.	A		17.	B
8.	C		18.	D
9.	B		19.	C
10.	A		20.	D

21. C
22. D
23. C
24. A
25. B

EXAMINATION SECTION
TEST 1

DIRECTIONS: Each question or incomplete statement is followed by several suggested answers or completions. Select the one that BEST answers the question or completes the statement. *PRINT THE LETTER OF THE CORRECT ANSWER IN THE SPACE AT THE RIGHT.*

1. For a large public park and recreation department, it is generally agreed that the key to productivity is 1.____

    A. contracting and leasing arrangements
    B. the effective management of personnel
    C. cost-benefit analysis
    D. appealing to private foundations for funds

2. In a park and recreation setting, four conditions must be present in a situation in order for the department to be found legally negligent, and therefore liable, in the case of an accident. Which of the following is NOT one of these conditions? 2.____

    A. Proof of injury or damage
    B. Legal responsibility for the participant
    C. The participant's lack of an employment relationship to the department
    D. The department's failure to take reasonable care

3. In a park and recreation department, the MOST effective approach to problem-solving is generally described as 3.____

    A. group-centered
    B. authoritarian
    C. decisions by higher authorities
    D. an analysis by planning specialists

4. Which of the following administration philosophies or strategies is part of the future-oriented trend in park and recreation management? 4.____

    A. Planning programs with the staff, chiefly by updating past programs
    B. Evaluating outcomes primarily through attendance figures
    C. Providing programs and services based on social and economic needs of the community
    D. Requiring financial accountability and justifying budgets based on historical precedent

5. The _____ approach to leisure service sees recreation as an important community service that is carried on both for its own sake and because it contributes to the mental and physical health of participants. 5.____

    A. human-services   B. prescriptive
    C. environmental   D. quality-of-life

6. More or increased _____ is NOT a growing trend in leisure services. 6.____

    A. centralized personnel structure
    B. emphasis on health and fitness

C. consideration of leisure's contribution to quality of life
D. emphasis on noncompetitive forms of play

7. The MOST common means of financing public recreation and park departments is through

   A. bonds
   B. grants
   C. taxes
   D. fees and charges

8. For evaluating the effectiveness of specific programs offered by a park and recreation department, each of the following methods is commonly used EXCEPT

   A. systems-based, goal-achievement models
   B. internal auditing by top management
   C. staff-based evaluation processes
   D. participant-based evaluation

9. A public agency that favors the delegation of authority is BEST described as

   A. heterogeneous
   B. decentralized
   C. individualistic
   D. irresponsible

10. The ability to _____ is NOT generally considered to be a core process that an entry-level employee in a park and recreation department should master.

    A. carry out both program planning and organizational planning
    B. formally articulate resource needs
    C. utilize leadership processes
    D. teach

11. A _____ budget is designed in such a way that large units of work, or special programs, are isolated, identified, and described in detail.

    A. object classification
    B. function classification
    C. program
    D. performance

12. When programming recreational activities for participants in middle childhood (6-12 years), it is important to remember that they are generally

    A. preferring separation into sexually segregated groups
    B. physically aggressive
    C. physically growing more quickly than in preschool years
    D. unconcerned about ideas such as competence, achievement, and approval from others

13. Of the following issues, _____ is LEAST likely to be negotiated in a park and recreation labor union contractual agreement.

    A. work hours
    B. contracting work, or *outsourcing*
    C. safety regulations
    D. retirement plans

14. Which of the following is considered to be the responsibility of an auxiliary staff member at a park and recreation department?   14._____

    A. Supervision of sport programs
    B. Monitoring adherence to agency rules
    C. Direction of administrative guidelines
    D. Organizing sport activities

15. Traditionally, leisure facilities have been planned according to   15._____

    A. concepts of the neighborhood and community
    B. urban planning methods based on land-use principles
    C. a needs index
    D. recommended standards of open space

16. Public agencies such as park and recreation departments typically use one of several contemporary models in evaluating whether the agency has achieved its stated objectives. Which of the following is NOT one of these models?
    Evaluation designed to measure the   16._____

    A. overall quality of programs, based on the opinion of an advisory board
    B. effectiveness of programs in meeting their stated goals and objectives
    C. effectiveness of personnel in carrying out stated program goals and objectives
    D. level of satisfaction of program participants

17. It is NOT typically a function of a public park and recreation agency's board or commission to   17._____

    A. review and approve all policies and work with the agency's managers to develop plans for meeting present and future leisure needs of the community
    B. consider and approve all personnel appointments or promotions
    C. articulate to the agency's director and staff how the details of administration should be carried out
    D. carry out long-range planning in cooperation with other community organizations to meet public recreational needs

18. In handling employment inquiries, application forms, and interviews for employment, questions to the applicant about _____ may be allowed under law, whether their use is job-related or not.   18._____

    A. employment history
    B. physical requirements
    C. arrest and conviction record
    D. age

19. According to most current practices in public agencies, any overspending or underspending in the year's budget is to be brought to the department head's attention in the month of   19._____

    A. January   B. February
    C. March or April   D. November

20. In order to avoid legal liability for certain activities involving children, some park and recreation departments use the convention of permission slips signed by a parent or guardian, in which they are asked to waive the right to sue in case of injury or accident. For several reasons, these slips offer the department a false sense of security. Which of the following is NOT one of these reasons?

    I. In all cases, signed statements are invalid if the risks of the activity are not understood.
    II. The waiver is not valid unless signed by both parents, no matter what their geographic location.
    III. They cannot waive the right of a child to bring suit against the agency when the child reaches the legal age for doing so.

    The CORRECT answer is:

    A. I only   B. I, II   C. I, III   D. I, II, III

21. Which of the following recreation facilities would most likely be located at or near the intersection of major or secondary thoroughfares near the center of a 4- or 5-square mile service area?

    A. Playlot
    B. Large park
    C. Playground
    D. Athletic field

22. Which of the following is NOT a level of planning commonly associated with recreation and park facilities?

    A. Planning that focuses solely on recreation and park development within a total community, sometimes as a separate portion of a total plan
    B. Regional planning that takes into account services and facilities offered by adjacent jurisdictions
    C. Planning that is concerned with the development of a particular facility or the needs of a single neighborhood
    D. Total master planning that considers all aspects of municipal growth, including industrial and residential development, transportation, education, housing, health, etc.

23. The MAIN advantage of a structured, centralized approach to recreational programming is

    A. being able to respond to local neighborhood needs
    B. optimum legal protection from liability claims
    C. more efficient use of personnel resources
    D. a set of clear-cut standards for fulfilling the agency's stated objectives

24. When programming recreational activities for participants in middle adulthood (40-65 years), it is important to remember that they generally

    A. experience physiological changes in the brain
    B. begin to experience instability in cognitive skills
    C. display a loss of creativity
    D. tend to gain weight easily

25. In park and recreation accounting, concurrent auditing represents   25._____
    A. a preaudit of expected income or disbursements
    B. a formal check of specific administrative or program divisions of a department, or construction or maintenance projects
    C. a form of bookkeeping report showing the assets and liabilities of a given fund or budget
    D. all departmental expenditures that have been authorized and carried out

KEY (CORRECT ANSWERS)

1. B
2. C
3. A
4. C
5. D

6. A
7. C
8. B
9. B
10. B

11. C
12. A
13. B
14. A
15. C

16. A
17. C
18. A
19. B
20. C

21. D
22. B
23. D
24. D
25. A

TEST 2

DIRECTIONS: Each question or incomplete statement is followed by several suggested answers or completions. Select the one that BEST answers the question or completes the statement. *PRINT THE LETTER OF THE CORRECT ANSWER IN THE SPACE AT THE RIGHT.*

1. Each of the following is a benefit associated with the use of a *matrix* structure in a public park and recreation department EXCEPT   1.____

    A. greater opportunity of employees' personal development
    B. better technical performance
    C. improved flexibility in conditions of change and uncertainty
    D. involvement in long-range planning of employees at every level

2. Which of the following statements about recreationists in early adulthood (20-39 years) is generally TRUE?   2.____

    A. They are more self-centered than adolescents.
    B. Their friendships are characterized by less intimacy.
    C. They experience a lack of stability in intellectual skills.
    D. They expand their social relationships through new contacts within the occupational and community settings.

3. When programming recreation activities, an administrator's choices are likely to be affected by each of the following factors EXCEPT   3.____

    A. the number of potential activities
    B. the characteristics of participants
    C. the funds required
    D. personnel

4. A recreation programmer wants to stage a single-elimination summer softball tournament at the department's facilities. Each of the following is an advantage associated with the single-elimination format EXCEPT it   4.____

    A. is usually more interesting for spectators
    B. may accommodate a large number of participants
    C. encourages maximum participation
    D. is the most economical to conduct

5. In a recreation or park facility's off-season, an administrator wants to maintain a minimum level of care. Typically, how often should litter at the facility be picked up?   5.____

    A. Daily   B. Weekly
    C. Monthly   D. Every two months

6. Funding agencies for public park and recreation departments have historically applied strict criteria for determining grant recipients. Which of the following statements about their considerations is generally FALSE?   6.____

    A. There must be evidence that existing programs and facilities are being fully utilized.
    B. Agencies applying for grants must be prepared to guarantee a substantial portion of the total grant proposal.

C. Higher priority is given to proposals that come from more than one agency or sponsor.
D. Wherever possible, grant proposals should be designed to serve the general population, rather than isolated or special-need communities.

7. In public recreation programs, sport accounts for about _____% of all active involvement.

   A. 10-30   B. 35-50   C. 60-75   D. 80-95

8. Which of the following is NOT a level of responsibility defined by the functional classification of personnel analysis?

   A. Managerial   B. Tutorial
   C. Logistical   D. Operational

9. During a community needs assessment, a park and recreation department would most likely conduct use surveys among the community members in order to determine the _____ leisure needs of the community.

   A. expressed   B. normative   C. relative   D. perceived

10. The main disadvantage to using an *object classification* type of budget for a park and recreation department is that

    A. it does not relate expenditures meaningfully to programs
    B. certain expenditures, such as personnel, are not considered *objects*
    C. it does not provide complete itemization of expenditures
    D. it does not take unplanned expenditures into account

11. Which of the following is NOT a guideline to follow in preparing a newspaper release for a public park and recreation department event or service?

    A. The release should stick to the facts and avoid editorializing.
    B. An attempt should be made to feature a prominent or interesting individual or group of people in the article.
    C. The most important information should be included at the beginning of the article.
    D. The release should be limited to 2 or 3 pages.

12. In a public school or college's recreational facilities, the priority of use must be

    A. intramural or campus recreational programming
    B. intercollegiate practice sessions or competition
    C. formal academic program use
    D. community residents

13. For a supervisor in a park and recreation department, each of the following is a guideline to follow in taking disciplinary action with employees EXCEPT

    A. when correction is required, it should be handled in private
    B. the worker should be told what he or she can do to correct the situation
    C. the action should not be taken until some time after the need for it has been established
    D. take the same corrective actions for the same behaviors with different individuals

14. The healthiest way a park and recreation department manager can approach the subject of inter-employee conflict is to view it as

    A. inevitable, but desirable and able to be used to constructive ends
    B. a healthy sign that workers in the department intend to challenge and compete with one another to meet departmental goals
    C. an inevitable product of a close working relationship that should be not denied, but endured peaceably
    D. a harmful and destructive influence that should be avoided at all costs

15. Which of the following is NOT generally considered to be a guideline to follow in determining when, and for what, recreation fees and charges are justified?

    A. Frequently charge where *preservation* is the dominant function
    B. Be sure that some benefit accrues to the taxpayer
    C. The specific services to be charged for and the fee should be matters of local choice
    D. Frequently charge where *use* is the dominant function

16. Generally, which of the following approaches to urban planning is used LEAST often?

    A. Developing an ideal model of the community
    B. Cost-revenue model
    C. User-oriented approach
    D. Needs index model

17. When conditions within a working group are only moderately favorable or unfavorable (i.e., the leader is well-liked but the task under consideration is unstructured), what type of leadership style is most appropriate?

    A. Laissez-faire   B. Task-oriented
    C. Authoritarian   D. Relationship-oriented

18. In a park and recreation department, a cost-benefit analysis is LEAST likely to be useful for

    A. identifying high- and low-cost programs and services as related to maintenance, administration, and direct leadership costs per participant-hour of service rendered
    B. providing valuable support data for justifying budget requests
    C. providing essential data for determining the cost-effectiveness of individual department personnel
    D. permitting the assignment of priorities to specific programs and services

19. In recent years, the number of volunteers working for public park and recreation departments has increased among certain segments of the population. Among the following groups, which has shown the LEAST significant increase in volunteer service?

    A. Females   B. Males
    C. Poor people   D. Minorities

20. The major type of legislation affecting parks and recreation is the

    A. regulatory law   B. special district law
    C. enabling law   D. home rule legislation

21. When programming recreational activities for participants in late adulthood (over 65 years), it is important to remember that they generally

    A. do not require a significant restructuring of time
    B. have a self-concept that tends to be more dependent upon external factors
    C. prefer to live in close contact with others of their age group
    D. become less active if they are men, and more active if they are women

22. The self-study approach to agency evaluation, outlined by the National Recreation and Park Association, includes standards that are used in measuring the effectiveness of a department in several major categories. Which of the following is NOT one of these categories?

    A. Administration   B. Evaluation
    C. Programming   D. Funding

23. Decisions made at the lower level of an agency's management, which are part of operational planning and program implementation, are described as _____ decisions.

    A. primary   B. problem-oriented
    C. reflex   D. task-oriented

24. In park and recreation applications, a *flowchart* is used to

    A. view the community-wide availability of programs and detect under- or over-provision of different types of activities on a geographical basis
    B. show all events or continuing activities in a convenient and easily understood form
    C. show individual projects or programs laid out along a calendar, with specific tasks indicated for the dates on which they are to be begun and completed
    D. identify major facilities and ongoing programs

25. In recreation and sports injury cases involving parents and children, the parents, but not the child, can be barred from recovery for a child's injury under certain conditions. Which of the following is NOT one of these conditions?
    The

    A. parent has failed to exercise reasonable care to prevent the child from placing himself in a situation in which lack of self-protective capacity may reasonably be expected to result in harm to the child
    B. child is too young to exercise self-protection
    C. child's incapacity is a contributing factor in harm
    D. injury involves an *attractive nuisance*

KEY (CORRECT ANSWERS)

1. D
2. D
3. A
4. C
5. A

6. D
7. C
8. B
9. D
10. A

11. D
12. C
13. C
14. A
15. A

16. B
17. D
18. C
19. A
20. C

21. D
22. D
23. D
24. C
25. D

RECORD KEEPING
EXAMINATION SECTION
TEST 1

DIRECTIONS: Each question or incomplete statement is followed by several suggested answers or completions. Select the one that BEST answers the question or completes the statement. *PRINT THE LETTER OF THE CORRECT ANSWER IN THE SPACE AT THE RIGHT.*

Questions 1-7.

DIRECTIONS: In answering Questions 1 through 7, use the following master list. For each question, determine where the name would fit on the master list. Each answer choice indicates right before or after the name in the answer choice.

> Aaron, Jane
> Armstead, Brendan
> Bailey, Charles
> Dent, Ricardo
> Grant, Mark
> Mars, Justin
> Methieu, Justine
> Parker, Cathy
> Sampson, Suzy
> Thomas, Heather

1. Schmidt, William
   A. Right before Cathy Parker
   B. Right after Heather Thomas
   C. Right after Suzy Sampson
   D. Right before Ricardo Dent

2. Asanti, Kendall
   A. Right before Jane Aaron
   B. Right after Charles Bailey
   C. Right before Justine Methieu
   D. Right after Brendan Armstead

3. O'Brien, Daniel
   A. Right after Justine Methieu
   B. Right before Jane Aaron
   C. Right after Mark Grant
   D. Right before Suzy Sampson

4. Marrow, Alison
   A. Right before Cathy Parker
   B. Right before Justin Mars
   C. Right before Mark Grant
   D. Right after Heather Thomas

5. Grantt, Marissa
   A. Right before Mark Grant
   B. Right after Mark Grant
   C. Right after Justin Mars
   D. Right before Suzy Sampson

1.____

2.____

3.____

4.____

5.____

59

6. Thompson, Heath
   A. Right after Justin Mars
   B. Right before Suzy Sampson
   C. Right after Heather Thomas
   D. Right before Cathy Parker

6.____

DIRECTIONS: Before answering Question 7, add in all of the names from Questions 1 through 6. Then fit the name in alphabetical order based on the new list.

7. Francisco, Mildred
   A. Right before Mark Grant
   B. Right after Marissa Grantt
   C. Right before Alison Marrow
   D. Right after Kendall Asanti

7.____

Questions 8-10.

DIRECTIONS: In answering Questions 8 through 10, compare each pair of names and addresses. Indicate whether they are the same or different in any way.

8. William H. Pratt, J.D.   William H. Pratt, J.D.
   Attourney at Law   Attorney at Law
   A. No differences
   B. 1 difference
   C. 2 differences
   D. 3 differences

8.____

9. 1303 Theater Drive,; Apt. 3-B   1330 Theatre Drive,; Apt. 3-B
   A. No differences
   B. 1 difference
   C. 2 differences
   D. 3 differences

9.____

10. Petersdorff, Briana and Mary   Petersdorff, Briana and Mary
    A. No differences
    B. 1 difference
    C. 2 differences
    D. 3 differences

10.____

11. Which of the following words, if any, are misspelled?
    A. Affordable
    B. Circumstansial
    C. Legalese
    D. None of the above

11.____

Questions 12-13.

DIRECTIONS: Questions 12 and 13 are to be answered on the basis of the following table.

Standardized Test Results for High School Students in District #1230

	English	Math	Science	Reading
High School 1	21	22	15	18
High School 2	12	16	13	15
High School 3	16	18	21	17
High School 4	19	14	15	16

The scores for each high school in the district were averaged out and listed for each subject tested. Scores of 0-10 are significantly below College Readiness Standards. 11-15 are below College Readiness, 16-20 meet College Readiness, and 21-25 are above College Readiness.

12. If the high schools need to meet or exceed in at least half the categories in order to NOT be considered "at risk," which schools are considered "at risk"? 12.____
    A. High School 2   B. High School 3
    C. High School 4   D. Both A and C

13. What percentage of subjects did the district as a whole meet or exceed College Readiness standards? 13.____
    A. 25%   B. 50%   C. 75%   D. 100%

Questions 14-15.

DIRECTIONS: Questions 14 and 15 are to be answered on the basis of the following information.

You have seven employees working as a part of your team: Austin, Emily, Jeremy, Christina, Martin, Harriet, and Steve. You have just sent an e-mail informing them that there will be a mandatory training session next week. To ensure that work still gets done, you are offering the training twice during the week: once on Tuesday and also on Thursday. This way half the employees will still be working while the other half attend the training. The only other issue is that Jeremy doesn't work on Tuesdays and Harriet doesn't work on Thursdays due to compressed work schedules.

14. Which of the following is a possible attendance roster for the first training session? 14.____
    A. Emily, Jeremy, Steve   B. Steve, Christina, Harriet
    C. Harriet, Jeremy, Austin   D. Steve, Martin, Jeremy

15. If Harriet, Christina, and Steve attend the training session on Tuesday, which of the following is a possible roster for Thursday's training session? 15.____
    A. Jeremy, Emily, and Austin   B. Emily, Martin, and Harriet
    C. Austin, Christina, and Emily   D. Jeremy, Emily, and Steve

Questions 16-20.

DIRECTIONS: In answering Questions 16 through 20, you will be given a word and will need to choose the answer choice that is MOST similar or different to the word.

16. Which word means the SAME as *annual*? 16.____
    A. Monthly   B. Usually   C. Yearly   D. Constantly

17. Which word means the SAME as *effort*? 17.____
    A. Energy   B. Equate   C. Cherish   D. Commence

18. Which word means the OPPOSITE of *forlorn*? 18.____
    A. Neglected B. Lethargy   C. Optimistic D. Astonished

19. Which word means the SAME as *risk*? 19.____
    A. Admire   B. Hazard   C. Limit   D. Hesitant

20. Which word means the OPPOSITE of *translucent*?
    A. Opaque   B. Transparent   C. Luminous   D. Introverted

21. Last year, Jamie's annual salary was $50,000. Her boss called her today to inform her that she would receive a 20% raise for the upcoming year. How much more money will Jamie receive next year?
    A. $60,000   B. $10,000   C. $1,000   D. $51,000

22. You and a co-worker work for a temp hiring agency as part of their office staff. You both are given 6 days off per month. How many days off are you and your co-worker given in a year?
    A. 24   B. 72   C. 144   D. 48

23. If Margot makes $34,000 per year and she works 40 hours per week for all 52 weeks, what is her hourly rate?
    A. $16.34/hour   B. $17.00/hour   C. $15.54/hour   D. $13.23/hour

24. How many dimes are there in $175.00?
    A. 175   B. 1,750   C. 3,500   D. 17,500

25. If Janey is three times as old as Emily, and Emily is 3, how old is Janey?
    A. 6   B. 9   C. 12   D. 15

KEY (CORRECT ANSWERS)

1. C
2. D
3. A
4. B
5. B

6. C
7. A
8. B
9. C
10. A

11. B
12. A
13. D
14. B
15. A

16. C
17. A
18. C
19. B
20. A

21. B
22. C
23. A
24. B
25. B

TEST 2

DIRECTIONS: Each question or incomplete statement is followed by several suggested answers or completions. Select the one that BEST answers the question or completes the statement. *PRINT THE LETTER OF THE CORRECT ANSWER IN THE SPACE AT THE RIGHT.*

Questions 1-6.

DIRECTIONS: Questions 1 through 6 are to be answered on the basis of the following information.

item	name of item to be ordered
quantity	minimum number that can be ordered
beginning amount	amount in stock at start of month
amount received	amount receiving during month
ending amount	amount in stock at end of month
amount used	amount used during month
amount to order	will need at least as much of each item as used in the previous month
unit price	cost of each unit of an item
total price	total price for the order

Item	Quantity	Beginning	Received	Ending	Amount Used	Amount to Order	Unit Price	Total Price
Pens	10	22	10	8	24	20	$0.11	$2.20
Spiral notebooks	8	30	13	12			$0.25	
Binder clips	2 boxes	3 boxes	1 box	1 box			$1.79	
Sticky notes	3 packs	12 packs	4 packs	2 packs			$1.29	
Dry erase markers	1 pack (dozen)	34 markers	8 markers	40 markers			$16.49	
Ink cartridges (printer)	1 cartridge	3 cartridges	1 cartridge	2 cartridges			$79.99	
Folders	10 folders	25 folders	15 folders	10 folders			$1.08	

1. How many packs of sticky notes were used during the month? 1.____
   A. 16 B. 10 C. 12 D. 14

2. How many folders need to be ordered for next month? 2.____
   A. 15 B. 20 C. 30 D. 40

3. What is the total price of notebooks that you will need to order? 3.____
   A. $6.00 B. $0.25 C. $4.50 D. $2.75

4. Which of the following will you spend the second most money on? 4.____
   A. Ink cartridges B. Dry erase markers
   C. Sticky notes D. Binder clips

5. How many packs of dry erase markers should you order? 5.____
   A. 1 B. 8 C. 12 D. 0

6. What will be the total price of the file folders you order?   6.____
   A. $20.16   B. $21.60   C. $10.80   D. $4.32

Questions 7-11.

DIRECTIONS: Questions 7 through 11 are to be answered on the basis of the following table.

Number of Car Accidents, By Location and Cause, for 2014						
	Location 1		Location 2		Location 3	
Cause	Number	Percent	Number	Percent	Number	Percent
Severe Weather	10		25		30	
Excessive Speeding	20	40	5		10	
Impaired Driving	15		15	25	8	
Miscellaneous	5		15		2	4
TOTALS	50	100	60	100	50	100

7. Which of the following is the third highest cause of accidents for all three locations?   7.____
   A. Severe Weather   B. Impaired Driving
   C. Miscellaneous   D. Excessive Speeding

8. The average number of Severe Weather accidents per week at Location 3 for the year (52 weeks) was MOST NEARLY   8.____
   A. 0.57   B. 30   C. 1   D. 1.25

9. Which location had the LARGEST percentage of accidents caused by Impaired Driving?   9.____
   A. 1   B. 2   C. 3   D. Both A and B

10. If one-third of the accidents at all three locations resulted in at least one fatality, what is the LEAST amount of deaths caused by accidents last year?   10.____
    A. 60   B. 106   C. 66   D. 53

11. What is the percentage of accidents caused by miscellaneous means from all three locations in 2014?   11.____
    A. 5%   B. 10%   C. 13%   D. 25%

12. How many pairs of the following groups of letters are exactly alike?   12.____
    ACDOBJ   ACDBOJ
    HEWBWR   HEWRWB
    DEERVS   DEERVS
    BRFQSX   BRFQSX
    WEYRVB   WEYRVB
    SPQRZA   SQRPZA

    A. 2   B. 3   C. 4   D. 5

Questions 13-19.

DIRECTIONS: Questions 13 through 19 are to be answered on the basis of the following information.

In 2012, the most current information on the American population was finished. The information was compiled by 200 volunteers in each of the 50 states. The territory of Puerto Rico, a sovereign of the United States, had 25 people assigned to compile data. In February of 2010, volunteers in each state and sovereign began collecting information. In Puerto Rico, data collection finished by January 31st, 2011, while work in the United States was completed on June 30, 2012. Each volunteer gathered data on the population of their state or sovereign. When the information was compiled, volunteers sent reports to the nation's capital, Washington, D.C. Each volunteer worked 20 hours per month and put together 10 reports per month. After the data was compiled in total, 50 people reviewed the data and worked from January 2012 to December 2012.

13. How many reports were generated from February 2010 to April 2010 in Illinois and Ohio?
    A. 3,000   B. 6,000   C. 12,000   D. 15,000

14. How many volunteers in total collected population data in January 2012?
    A. 10,000   B. 2,000   C. 225   D. 200

15. How many reports were put together in May 2012?
    A. 2,000   B. 50,000   C. 100,000   D. 100,250

16. How many hours did the Puerto Rican volunteers work in the fall (September-November)?
    A. 60   B. 500   C. 1,500   D. 0

17. How many workers were compiling or reviewing data in July 2012?
    A. 25   B. 50   C. 200   D. 250

18. What was the total amount of hours worked by Nevada volunteers in July 2010?
    A. 500   B. 4,000   C. 4,500   D. 5,000

19. How many reviewers worked in January 2013?
    A. 75   B. 50   C. 0   D. 25

20. John has to file 10 documents per shelf. How many documents would it take for John to fill 40 shelves?
    A. 40   B. 400   C. 4,500   D. 5,000

21. Jill wants to travel from New York City to Los Angeles by bike, which is approximately 2,772 miles. How many miles per day would Jill need to average if she wanted to complete the trip in 4 weeks?
    A. 100   B. 89   C. 99   D. 94

4 (#2)

22. If there are 24 CPU's and only 7 monitors, how many more monitors do you need to have the same amount of monitors as CPU's?
    A. Not enough information
    B. 17
    C. 31
    D. 0

    22.____

23. If Gerry works 5 days a week and 8 hours each day, and John works 3 days a week and 10 hours each day, how many more hours per year will Gerry work than John?
    A. They work the same amount of hours.
    B. 450
    C. 520
    D. 832

    23.____

24. Jimmy gets transferred to a new office. The new office has 25 employees, but only 16 are there due to a blizzard. How many coworkers was Jimmy able to meet on his first day?
    A. 16   B. 25   C. 9   D. 7

    24.____

25. If you do a fundraiser for charities in your area and raise $500 total, how much would you give to each charity if you were donating equal amounts to 3 of them?
    A. $250.00   B. $167.77   C. $50.00   D. $111.11

    25.____

KEY (CORRECT ANSWERS)

1.	D		11.	C
2.	B		12.	B
3.	A		13.	C
4.	C		14.	A
5.	D		15.	C
6.	B		16.	C
7.	D		17.	B
8.	A		18.	B
9.	A		19.	C
10.	D		20.	B

21.	C
22.	B
23.	C
24.	A
25.	B

TEST 3

DIRECTIONS: Each question or incomplete statement is followed by several suggested answers or completions. Select the one that BEST answers the question or completes the statement. *PRINT THE LETTER OF THE CORRECT ANSWER IN THE SPACE AT THE RIGHT.*

Questions 1-3.

DIRECTIONS: In answering Questions 1 through 3, choose the correctly spelled word.

1. A. allusion   B. alusion   C. allusien   D. allution   1.____

2. A. altitude   B. alltitude   C. atlitude   D. altlitude   2.____

3. A. althogh   B. allthough   C. althrough   D. although   3.____

Questions 4-9.

DIRECTIONS: In answering Questions 4 through 9, choose the answer that BEST completes the analogy.

4. Odometer is to mileage as compass is to   4.____
    A. speed   B. needle   C. hiking   D. direction

5. Marathon is to race as hibernation is to   5.____
    A. winter   B. dream   C. sleep   D. bear

6. Cup is to coffee as bowl is to   6.____
    A. dish   B. spoon   C. food   D. soup

7. Flow is to river as stagnant is to   7.____
    A. pool   B. rain   C. stream   D. canal

8. Paw is to cat as hoof is to   8.____
    A. lamb   B. horse   C. lion   D. elephant

9. Architect is to building as sculptor is to   9.____
    A. museum   B. chisel   C. stone   D. statue

Questions 10-14.

DIRECTIONS: Questions 10 through 14 are to be answered on the basis of the following graph.

Population of Carroll City Broken Down by Age and Gender (in Thousands)			
Age	Female	Male	Total
Under 15	60	60	120
15-23		22	
24-33		20	44
34-43	13	18	31
44-53	20		67
64 and Over	65	65	130
TOTAL	230	232	462

10. How many people in the city are between the ages of 15-23?
    A. 70   B. 46,000   C. 70,000   D. 225,000

11. Approximately what percentage of the total population of the city was female aged 24-33?
    A. 10%   B. 5%   C. 15%   D. 25%

12. If 33% of the males have a job and 55% of females don't have a job, which of the following statements is TRUE?
    A. Males have approximately 2,600 more jobs than females.
    B. Females have approximately 49,000 more jobs than males.
    C. Females have approximately 26,000 more jobs than males.
    D. None of the above statements are true.

13. How many females between the ages of 15-23 live in Carroll City?
    A. 67,000   B. 24,000   C. 48,000   D. 91,000

14. Assume all males 44-53 living in Carroll City are employed. If two-thirds of males age 44-53 work jobs outside of Carroll City, how many work within city limits?
    A. 31,333
    B. 15,667
    C. 47,000
    D. Cannot answer the question with the information provided

10.____

11.____

12.____

13.____

14.____

Questions 15-16.

DIRECTIONS: Questions 15 and 16 are labeled as shown. Alphabetize them for filing. Choose the answer that correctly shows the order.

15. (1) AED
    (2) OOS
    (3) FOA
    (4) DOM
    (5) COB

    A. 2-5-4-3-2   B. 1-4-5-2-3   C. 1-5-4-2-3   D. 1-5-4-3-2

16. Alphabetize the names of the people. Last names are given last.
    (1) Lindsey Jamestown
    (2) Jane Alberta
    (3) Ally Jamestown
    (4) Allison Johnston
    (5) Lyle Moreno

    A. 2-1-3-4-5   B. 3-4-2-1-5   C. 2-3-1-4-5   D. 4-3-2-1-5

17. Which of the following words is misspelled?
    A. disgust
    B. whisper
    C. locale
    D. none of the above

Questions 18-21.

DIRECTIONS: Questions 18 through 21 are to be answered on the basis of the following list of employees.

    Robertson, Aaron
    Bacon, Gina
    Jerimiah, Trace
    Gillette, Stanley
    Jacks, Sharon

18. Which employee name would come in third in alphabetized list?
    A. Robertson, Aaron
    B. Jerimiah, Trace
    C. Gillette, Stanley
    D. Jacks, Sharon

19. Which employee's first name starts with the letter in the alphabet that is five letters after the first letter of their last name?
    A. Jerimiah, Trace
    B. Bacon, Gina
    C. Jacks, Sharon
    D. Gillette, Stanley

20. How many employees have last names that are exactly five letters long?
    A. 1   B. 2   C. 3   D. 4

4 (#3)

21. How many of the employees have either a first or last name that starts with the letter "G"? 21.____
   A. 1 B. 2 C. 4 D. 5

Questions 22-25.

DIRECTIONS: Questions 22 through 25 are to be answered on the basis of the following chart.

Bicycle Sales (Model #34JA32)							
Country	May	June	July	August	September	October	Total
Germany	34	47	45	54	56	60	296
Britain	40	44	36	47	47	46	260
Ireland	37	32	32	32	34	33	200
Portugal	14	14	14	16	17	14	89
Italy	29	29	28	31	29	31	177
Belgium	22	24	24	26	25	23	144
Total	176	198	179	206	208	207	1166

22. What percentage of the overall total was sold to the German importer? 22.____
   A. 25.3% B. 22% C. 24.1% D. 23%

23. What percentage of the overall total was sold in September? 23.____
   A. 24.1% B. 25.6% C. 17.9% D. 24.6%

24. What is the average number of units per month imported into Belgium over the first four months shown? 24.____
   A. 26 B. 20 C. 24 D. 31

25. If you look at the three smallest importers, what is their total import percentage? 25.____
   A. 35.1% B. 37.1% C. 40% D. 28%

KEY (CORRECT ANSWERS)

1.	A		11.	B
2.	A		12.	C
3.	D		13.	C
4.	D		14.	B
5.	C		15.	D
6.	D		16.	C
7.	A		17.	D
8.	B		18.	D
9.	D		19.	B
10.	C		20.	B

21. B
22. A
23. C
24. C
25. A

TEST 4

DIRECTIONS: Each question or incomplete statement is followed by several suggested answers or completions. Select the one that BEST answers the question or completes the statement. *PRINT THE LETTER OF THE CORRECT ANSWER IN THE SPACE AT THE RIGHT.*

Questions 1-6.

DIRECTIONS: In answering Questions 1 through 6, choose the sentence that represents the BEST example of English grammar.

1. A. Joey and me want to go on a vacation next week.
   B. Gary told Jim he would need to take some time off.
   C. If turning six years old, Jim's uncle would teach Spanish to him.
   D. Fax a copy of your resume to Ms. Perez and me.

2. A. Jerry stood in line for almost two hours.
   B. The reaction to my engagement was less exciting than I thought it would be.
   C. Carlos and me have done great work on this project.
   D. Two parts of the speech needs to be revised before tomorrow.

3. A. Arriving home, the alarm was tripped.
   B. Jonny is regarded as a stand up guy, a responsible parent, and he doesn't give up until a task is finished.
   C. Each employee must submit a drug test each month.
   D. One of the documents was incinerated in the explosion.

4. A. As soon as my parents get home, I told them I finished all of my chores.
   B. I asked my teacher to send me my missing work, check my absences, and how did I do on my test.
   C. Matt attempted to keep it concealed from Jenny and me.
   D. If Mary or him cannot get work done on time, I will have to split them up.

5. A. Driving to work, the traffic report warned him of an accident on Highway 47.
   B. Jimmy has performed well this season.
   C. Since finishing her degree, several job offers have been given to Cam.
   D. Our boss is creating unstable conditions for we employees.

6. A. The thief was described as a tall man with a wiry mustache weighing approximately 150 pounds.
   B. She gave Patrick and I some more time to finish our work.
   C. One of the books that he ordered was damaged in shipping.
   D. While talking on the rotary phone, the car Jim was driving skidded off the road.

2 (#4)

Questions 7-9.

DIRECTIONS: Questions 7 through 9 are to be answered on the basis of the following graph.

Ice Lake Frozen Flight (2002-2013)		
Year	Number of Participants	Temperature (Fahrenheit)
2002	22	4°
2003	50	33°
2004	69	18°
2005	104	22°
2006	108	24°
2007	288	33°
2008	173	9°
2009	598	39°
2010	698	26°
2011	696	30°
2012	777	28°
2013	578	32°

7. Which two year span had the LARGEST difference between temperatures? 7.____
   A. 2002 and 2003
   B. 2011 and 2012
   C. 2008 and 2009
   D. 2003 and 2004

8. How many total people participated in the years after the temperature reached at least 29°? 8.____
   A. 2,295   B. 1,717   C. 2,210   D. 4,543

9. In 2007, the event saw 288 participants, while in 2008 that number dropped to 173. Which of the following reasons BEST explains the drop in participants? 9.____
   A. The event had not been going on that long and people didn't know about it.
   B. The lake water wasn't cold enough to have people jump in.
   C. The temperature was too cold for many people who would have normally participated.
   D. None of the above reasons explain the drop in participants.

10. In the following list of numbers, how many times does 4 come just after 2 when 2 comes just after an odd number? 10.____
    2365247653898632488572486392424
    A. 2   B. 3   C. 4   D. 5

11. Which choice below lists the letter that is as far after B as S is after N in the alphabet? 11.____
    A. G   B. H   C. I   D. J

Questions 12-15.

DIRECTIONS: Questions 12 through 15 are to be answered on the basis of the following directory and list of changes.

Directory		
Name	Emp. Type	Position
Julie Taylor	Warehouse	Packer
James King	Office	Administrative Assistant
John Williams	Office	Salesperson
Ray Moore	Warehouse	Maintenance
Kathleen Byrne	Warehouse	Supervisor
Amy Jones	Office	Salesperson
Paul Jonas	Office	Salesperson
Lisa Wong	Warehouse	Loader
Eugene Lee	Office	Accountant
Bruce Lavine	Office	Manager
Adam Gates	Warehouse	Packer
Will Suter	Warehouse	Packer
Gary Lorper	Office	Accountant
Jon Adams	Office	Salesperson
Susannah Harper	Office	Salesperson

Directory Updates:
- Employee e-mail addresses will adhere to the following guidelines: lastnamefirstname@apexindustries.com (ex. Susannah Harper is harpersusannah@apexindustries.com). Currently, employees in the warehouse share one e-mail, distribution@apexindustries.com.
- The "Loader" position will now be referred to as "Specialist I"
- Adam Gates has accepted a Supervisor position within the Warehouse and is no longer a Packer. All warehouse employees report to the two Supervisors and all office employees report to the Manager.

12. Amy Jones tried to send an e-mail to Adam Gates, but it wouldn't send. Which of the following offers the BEST explanation?
    A. Amy put Adam's first name first and then his last name.
    B. Adam doesn't check his e-mail, so he wouldn't know if he received the e-mail or not.
    C. Adam does not have his own e-mail.
    D. Office employees are not allowed to send e-mails to each other.

13. How many Packers currently work for Apex Industries?
    A. 2   B. 3   C. 4   D. 5

14. What position does Lisa Wong currently hold?
    A. Specialist I   B. Secretary
    C. Administrative Assistant   D. Loader

15. If an employee wanted to contact the office manager, which of the following e-mails should the e-mail be sent to? 15.____
    A. officemanager@apexindustries.com
    B. brucelavine@apexindustries.com
    C. lavinebruce@apexindustries.com
    D. distribution@apexindustries.com

Questions 16-19.

DIRECTIONS: In answering Questions 16 through 19, compare the three names, numbers or addresses.

16. Smiley Yarnell   Smiley Yarnel   Smily Yarnell   16.____
    A. All three are exactly alike.
    B. The first and second are exactly alike.
    C. The second and third are exactly alike.
    D. All three are different.

17. 1583 Theater Drive   1583 Theater Drive   1583 Theatre Drive   17.____
    A. All three are exactly alike.
    B. The first and second are exactly alike.
    C. The second and third are exactly alike.
    D. All three are different.

18. 3341893212   3341893212   3341893212   18.____
    A. All three are exactly alike.
    B. The first and second are exactly alike.
    C. The second and third are exactly alike.
    D. All three are different.

19. Douglass Watkins   Douglas Watkins   Douglass Watkins   19.____
    A. All three are exactly alike.
    B. The first and third are exactly alike.
    C. The second and third are exactly alike.
    D. All three are different.

Questions 20-24.

DIRECTIONS: In answering Questions 20 through 24, you will be presented with a word. Choose the synonym that BEST represents the word in question.

20. Flexible   20.____
    A. delicate   B. inflammable   C. strong   D. pliable

21. Alternative   21.____
    A. choice   B. moderate   C. lazy   D. value

22. Corroborate
    A. examine   B. explain   C. verify   D. explain   22.____

23. Respiration
    A. recovery   B. breathing   C. sweating   D. selfish   23.____

24. Negligent
    A. lazy   B. moderate   C. hopeless   D. lax   24.____

25. Plumber is to Wrench as Painter is to   25.____
    A. pipe   B. shop   C. hammer   D. brush

KEY (CORRECT ANSWERS)

1. D
2. A
3. D
4. C
5. B

6. C
7. C
8. B
9. C
10. C

11. A
12. C
13. A
14. A
15. C

16. D
17. B
18. A
19. B
20. D

21. A
22. C
23. B
24. D
25. D

EXAMINATION SECTION

TEST 1

DIRECTIONS: Each question or incomplete statement is followed by several suggested answers or completions. Select the one that BEST answers the question or completes the statement. *PRINT THE LETTER OF THE CORRECT ANSWER IN THE SPACE AT THE RIGHT.*

1. Good procedure in handling complaints from the public may be divided into the following four principal stages:
   I. Investigation of the complaint
   II. Receipt of the complaint
   III. Assignment of responsibility for investigation and correction
   IV. Notification of correction

   The ORDER in which these stages ordinarily come is:
   A. III, II, I, IV   B. II, III, I, IV   C. II, III, IV, I   D. II, IV, III, I

   1.____

2. The department may expect the MOST severe public criticism if
   A. it asks for an increase in its annual budget
   B. it purchases new and costly street cleaning equipment
   C. sanitation officers and men are reclassified to higher salary grades
   D. there is delay in cleaning streets of snow

   2.____

3. The MOST important function of public relations in the department should be to
   A. develop cooperation on the part of the public in keeping streets clean
   B. get stricter penalties enacted for health code violations
   C. recruit candidates for entrance positions who ca be developed into supervisors
   D. train career personnel so that they can advance in the department

   3.____

4. The one of the following which has MOST frequently elicited unfavorable public comment has been
   A. dirty sidewalks or streets   B. dumping on lot
   C. failure to curb dogs   D. overflowing garbage cans

   4.____

5. It has been suggested that, as a public relations measure, sections hold *open house* for the public.
   The MOST effective time for this would be
   A. during the summer when children are not in school and can accompany their parents
   B. during the winter when show is likely to fall and the public can see snow removal preparations
   C. immediately after a heavy snow storm when department snow removal operations are in full progress
   D. when street sanitation is receiving general attention as during *Keep City Clean* week

   5.____

6. When a public agency conducts a public relations program, it is MOST likely to find that each recipient of its message will
   A. disagree with the basic purpose of the message if the officials are not well known to him
   B. accept the message if it is presented by someone perceived as having a definite intention to persuade
   C. ignore the message unless it is presented in a literate and clever manner
   D. give greater attention to certain portions of the message as a result of his individual and cultural differences

7. Following are three statements about public relations and communications:
   I. A person who seeks to influence public opinion can speed up a trend
   II. Mass communications is the exposure of a mass audience to an idea
   III. All media are equally effective in reaching opinion leaders
   Which of the following choices CORRECTLY classifies the above statements into those which are correct and those which are not?
   A. I and II are correct, but III is not.
   B. II and III are correct, but I is not.
   C. I and III are correct, but II is not.
   D. III is correct, but I and II are not.

8. Public relations experts say that MAXIMUM effect for a message results from
   A. concentrating in one medium
   B. ignoring mass media and concentrating on *opinion makers*
   C. presenting only those factors which support a given position
   D. using a combination of two or more of the available media

9. To assure credibility and avoid hostility, the public relations man MUST
   A. make certain his message is truthful, not evasive or exaggerated
   B. make sure his message contains some dire consequence if ignored
   C. repeat the message often enough so that it cannot be ignored
   D. try to reach as many people and groups as possible

10. The public relations man MUST be prepared to assume that members of his audience
    A. may have developed attitudes toward his proposals—favorable, neutral, or unfavorable
    B. will be immediately hostile
    C. will consider his proposals with an open mind
    D. will invariably need an introduction to his subject

11. The one of the following statements that is CORRECT is:
    A. When a stupid question is asked of you by the public, it should be disregarded
    B. If you insist on formality between you and the public, the public will not be able to ask stupid questions that cannot be answered
    C. The public should be treated courteously, regardless of how stupid their questions may be
    D. You should explain to the public how stupid their questions are

12. With regard to public relations, the MOST important item which should be emphasized in an employee training program is that
    A. each inspector is a public relations agent
    B. an inspector should give the public all the information it asks for
    C. it is better to make mistakes and give erroneous information than to tell the public that you do not know the correct answer to their problem
    D. public relations is so specialized a field that only persons specially trained in it should consider it

13. Members of the public frequently ask about departmental procedures. Of the following, it is BEST to
    A. advise the public to put the question in writing so that he can get a proper formal reply
    B. refuse to answer because this is a confidential matter
    C. explain the procedure as briefly as possible
    D. attempt to avoid the issue by discussing other matters

14. The effectiveness of a public relations program in a public agency such as the authority is BEST indicated by the
    A. amount of mass media publicity favorable to the policies of the authority
    B. morale of those employees who directly serve the patrons of the authority
    C. public's understanding and support of the authority's program and policies
    D. number of complaint received by the authority from patrons using its facilities

15. In an attempt to improve public opinion about a certain idea, the BEST course of action for an agency to take would be to present the
    A. clearest statements of the idea even though the language is somewhat technical
    B. idea as the result of long-term studies
    C. idea in association with something familiar to most people
    D. idea as the viewpoint of the majority leaders

16. The fundamental factor in any agency's community relations program is
    A. an outline of the objectives
    B. relations with the media
    C. the everyday actions of the employees
    D. a well-planned supervisory program

17. The FUNDAMENTAL factor in the success of a community relations program is
    A. true commitment by the community
    B. true commitment by the administration
    C. a well-planned, systematic approach
    D. the actions of individuals in their contacts with the public

18. The statement below which is LEAST correct is:
    A. Because of selection standards, the supervisor frequently encounters problems resulting from subordinates' inability to express themselves in the language of the profession.
    B. Distortion of the meaning of a communication is usually brought about by a failure to use language that has a precise meaning to others.
    C. The term *filtering* is the distortion or dilution of content of a communication that occurs as information is passed from individual to individual.
    D. The complexity of the *communications net* will directly affect.

19. Consider the following three statements that may or may not be CORRECT:
    I. In order to prevent the stifling of communications flow, supervisors should insist that employees use the formal communications network.
    II. Two-way communications are faster and more accurate than one-way communications.
    III. There is a direct correlation between the effectiveness of communications and the total setting in which they occur.
    The choice below which MOST accurately describes the above statement is:
    A. All three are correct.
    B. All three are incorrect.
    C. More than one statement is correct.
    D. Only one of the statements is correct.

20. The statement below which is MOST inaccurate is:
    A. The supervisor's most important tool in learning whether or not he is communicating well is feedback.
    B. Follow-up is essential if useful feedback is to be obtained.
    C. Subordinates are entitled, as a matter of right, to explanations from management concerning the reasons for orders or directives.
    D. A skilled supervisor is often able to use the grapevine to good advantage.

21. *Since concurrence by those affected is not sought, this kind of communication can be issued with relative ease.*
    The kind of communication being referred to in this quotation is
    A. autocratic   B. democratic   C. directive   D. free-rein

22. The statement below which is LEAST correct is:
    A. Clarity is more important in oral communicating than in written since the readers of a written communication can read it over again.
    B. Excessive use of abbreviations in written communications should be avoided.
    C. Short sentences with simple words are preferred over complex sentences and difficult words in a written communication.
    D. The *newspaper* style of writing ordinarily simplifies expression and facilitates understanding.

23. Which one of the following is the MOST important factor for the department to consider in building a good public image?
    A. A good working relationship with the news media
    B. An efficient community relations program
    C. An efficient system for handling citizen complaints
    D. The proper maintenance of facilities and equipment
    E. The behavior of individuals in their contacts with the public.

24. It has been said that the ability to communicate clearly and concisely is the MOST important single skill of the supervisor.
    Consider the following statements:
    I.   The adage, *Actions speak louder than words*, has NO application in superior/subordinate communications since good communications are accomplished with words.
    II. The environment in which a communication takes place will *rarely* determine its effect.
    III. Words are symbolic representations which must be associated with past experience or else they are meaningless.
    The choice below which MOST accurately describes the above statements is:
    A. I, II, and III are correct.
    B. I and II are correct, but III is not.
    C. I and III are correct, but II is not.
    D. III is correct, but I and II are not.
    E. I, II, and III are incorrect.

25. According to expert opinion, the effectiveness of an organization is very dependent upon good upward, downward, and lateral communications. Lateral communications are most important to the activity of coordinating the efforts of organizational units. Before real communication can take place at any level, barriers to communication must be recognized, understood, and removed.
    Consider the following three statements:
    I.   The *principal* barrier to good communications is a failure to establish empathy between sender and receiver.
    II. The difference in status or rank between the sender and receiver of a communication may be a communications barrier.
    III. Communications are easier if they travel upward from subordinate to superior
    The choice below which MOST accurately describes the above statements is:
    A. I, II and III are incorrect.   B. I and II are incorrect.
    C. I, II, and III are correct.   D. I and II are correct.
    E. I and III are incorrect.

KEY (CORRECT ANSWERS)

1.	B		11.	C
2.	D		12.	A
3.	A		13.	C
4.	A		14.	C
5.	D		15.	C
6.	D		16.	C
7.	A		17.	D
8.	D		18.	A
9.	A		19.	D
10.	A		20.	C

21. A
22. A
23. E
24. D
25. E

EXAMINATION SECTION
TEST 1

DIRECTIONS: Each question or incomplete statement is followed by several suggested answers or completions. Select the one that BEST answers the question or completes the statement. *PRINT THE LETTER OF THE CORRECT ANSWER IN THE SPACE AT THE RIGHT.*

1. Which of the following is the MOST likely action a supervisor should take to help establish an effective working relationship with his departmental superiors?
   A. Delay the implementation of new procedures received from superiors in order to evaluate their appropriateness.
   B. Skip the chain of command whenever he feels that it is to his advantage
   C. Keep supervisors informed of problems in his area and the steps taken to correct them
   D. Don't take up superiors' time by discussing anticipated problems but wait until the difficulties occur

1.____

2. Of the following, the action a supervisor could take which would generally be MOST conducive to the establishment of an effective working relationship with employees includes
   A. maintaining impersonal relationships to prevent development of biased actions
   B. treating all employees equally without adjusting for individual differences
   C. continuous observation of employees on the job with insistence on constant improvement
   D. careful planning and scheduling of work for your employees

2.____

3. Which of the following procedures is the LEAST likely to establish effective working relationships between employees and supervisors?
   A. Encouraging two-way communication with employees
   B. Periodic discussion with employees regarding their job performance
   C. Ignoring employees' gripes concerning job difficulties
   D. Avoiding personal prejudices in dealing with employees

3.____

4. Criticism can be used as a tool to point out the weak areas of a subordinate's work performance.
Of the following, the BEST action for a supervisor to take so that his criticism will be accepted is to
   A. focus his criticism on the act instead of on the person
   B. exaggerate the errors in order to motivate the employee to do better
   C. pass judgment quickly and privately without investigating the circumstances of the error
   D. generalize the criticism and not specifically point out the errors in performance

4.____

5. In trying to improve the motivation of his subordinates, a supervisor can achieve the BEST results by taking action based upon the assumption that most employees
    A. have an inherent dislike of work
    B. wish to be closely directed
    C. are more interested in security than in assuming responsibility
    D. will exercise self-direction without coercion

6. When there are conflicts or tensions between top management and lower-level employees in any department, the supervisor should FIRST attempt to
    A. represent and enforce the management point of view
    B. act as the representative of the workers to get their ideas across to management
    C. serve as a two-way spokesman, trying to interpret each side to the other
    D. remain neutral, but keep informed of changes in the situation

7. A probationary period for new employees is usually provided in many agencies. The MAJOR purpose of such a period is usually to
    A. allow a determination of employee's suitability for the position
    B. obtain evidence as to employee's ability to perform in a higher position
    C. conform to requirements that ethnic hiring goals be met for all positions
    D. train the new employee in the duties of the position

8. An effective program of orientation for new employees usually includes all of the following EXCEPT
    A. having the supervisor introduce the new employee to his job, outlining his responsibilities and how to carry them out
    B. permitting the new worker to tour the facility or department so he can observe all parts of it in action
    C. scheduling meetings for new employees, at which the job requirements are explained to them and they are given personnel manuals
    D. testing the new worker on his skills and sending him to a centralized in-service workshop

9. In-service training is an important responsibility of many supervisors. The MAJOR reason for such training is to
    A. avoid future grievance procedures because employees might say they were not prepared to carry out their jobs
    B. maximize the effectiveness of the department by helping each employee perform at his full potential
    C. satisfy inspection teams from central headquarters of the department
    D. help prevent disagreements with members of the community

10. There are many forms of useful in-service training. Of the following, the training method which is NOT an appropriate technique for leadership development is to
    A. provide special workshops or clinics in activity skills
    B. conduct institutes to familiarize new workers with the program of the department and with their roles

C. schedule team meetings for problem-solving, including both supervisors and leaders
D. have the leader rate himself on an evaluation form periodically

11. Of the following techniques of evaluating work training programs, the one that is BEST is to
    A. pass out a carefully designed questionnaire to the trainees at the completion of the program
    B. test the knowledge that trainees have both at the beginning of training and at its completion
    C. interview the trainees at the completion of the program
    D. evaluate performance before and after training for both a control group and an experimental group

11._____

12. Assume that a new supervisor is having difficulty making his instructions to subordinates clearly understood.
    The one of the following which is the FIRST step he should take in dealing with this problem is to
    A. set up a training workshop in communication skills
    B. determine the extent and nature of the communications gap
    C. repeat both verbal and written instructions several times
    D. simplify his written and spoken vocabulary

12._____

13. A director has not properly carried out the orders of his assistant supervisor on several occasions to the point where he has been successively warned, reprimanded, and severely reprimanded.
    When the director once again does not carry out orders, the PROPER action for the assistant supervisor to take is to
    A. bring the director up on charges of failing to perform his duties properly
    B. have a serious discussion with the director, explaining the need for the orders and the necessity for carrying them out
    C. recommend that the director be transferred to another district
    D. severely reprimand the director again, making clear that no further deviation will be countenanced

13._____

14. A supervisor with several subordinates becomes aware that two of these subordinates are neither friendly nor congenial.
    In making assignments, it would be BEST for the supervisor to
    A. disregard the situation
    B. disregard the situation in making a choice of assignment but emphasize the need for teamwork
    C. investigate the situation to find out who is at fault and give that individual the less desirable assignments until such time as he corrects his attitude
    D. place the unfriendly subordinates in positions where they have as little contact with one another as possible

14._____

15. A DESIRABLE characteristic of a good supervisor is that he should   15.____
    A. identify himself with his subordinates rather than with higher management
    B. inform subordinates of forthcoming changes in policies and programs only when they directly affect the subordinates' activities
    C. make advancement of the subordinates contingent on personal loyalty to the supervisor
    D. make promises to subordinates only when sure of the ability to keep them

16. The supervisor who is MOST likely to be successful is the one who   16.____
    A. refrains from exercising the special privileges of his position
    B. maintains a formal attitude toward his subordinates
    C. maintains an informal attitude toward his subordinates
    D. represents the desires of his subordinate to his superiors

17. Application of sound principles of human relations by a supervisor may be expected to _____ the need for formal discipline.   17.____
    A. decrease   B. have no effect on
    C. increase   D. obviate

18. The MOST important generally approved way to maintain or develop high morale in one's subordinates is to   18.____
    A. give warnings and reprimands in a jocular way
    B. excuse from staff conferences those employees who are busy
    C. keep them informed of new developments and policies of higher management
    D. refrain from criticizing their faults directly

19. In training subordinates, an IMPORTANT principle for the supervisor to recognize is that   19.____
    A. a particular method of instruction will be of substantially equal value for all employees in a given title
    B. it is difficult to train people over 50 years of age because they have little capacity for learning
    C. persons undergoing the same course of training will learn at different rates of speed
    D. training can seldom achieve its purpose unless individual instruction is the chief method used

20. Over an extended period of time, a subordinate is MOST likely to become and remain most productive if the supervisor   20.____
    A. accords praise to the subordinate whenever his work is satisfactory, withholding criticism except in the case of very inferior work
    B. avoids both praise and criticism except for outstandingly good or bad work performed by the subordinate
    C. informs the subordinate of his shortcomings, as viewed by management, while according praise only when highly deserved
    D. keeps the subordinate informed of the degree of satisfaction with which his performance of the job is viewed by management.

KEY (CORRECT ANSWERS)

1.	C	11.	D
2.	D	12.	B
3.	C	13.	A
4.	A	14.	D
5.	D	15.	D
6.	C	16.	D
7.	A	17.	A
8.	D	18.	C
9.	B	19.	C
10.	D	20.	D

TEST 2

DIRECTIONS: Each question or incomplete statement is followed by several suggested answers or completions. Select the one that BEST answers the question or completes the statement. *PRINT THE LETTER OF THE CORRECT ANSWER IN THE SPACE AT THE RIGHT.*

1. A supervisor has just been told by a subordinate, Mr. Jones, that another employee, Mr. Smith, deliberately disobeyed an important rule of the department by taking home some confidential departmental material.
 Of the following courses of action, it would be MOST advisable for the supervisor FIRST to
   A. discuss the matter privately with both Mr. Jones and Mrs. Smith at the same time
   B. call a meeting of the entire staff and discuss the matter generally without mentioning any employee by name
   C. arrange to supervise Mr. Smith's activities more closely
   D. discuss the matter privately with Mr. Smith

2. The one of the following actions which would be MOST efficient and economical for a supervisor to take to minimize the effect of periodical fluctuations in the workload of his unit is to
   A. increase his permanent staff until it is large enough to handle the work of the busy loads
   B. request the purchase of time- and labor-saving equipment to be used primarily during the busy loads
   C. lower, temporarily, the standards for quality of work performance during peak loads
   D. schedule for the slow periods work that is not essential to perform during the busy periods

3. Discipline of employees is usually a supervisor's responsibility. There may be several useful forms of disciplinary action.
 Of the following, the form that is LEAST appropriate is the
   A. written reprimand or warning
   B. involuntary transfer to another work setting
   C. demotion or suspension
   D. assignment of added hours of work each week

4. Of the following, the MOST effective means of dealing with employee disciplinary problems is to
   A. give personality tests to individuals to identify their psychological problems
   B. distribute and discuss a policy manual containing exact rules governing employee behavior
   C. establish a single, clear penalty to be imposed for all wrongdoing irrespective of degree
   D. have supervisors get to know employees well through social mingling

5. A recently developed technique for appraising work performance is to have the supervisor record on a continual basis all significant incidents in each subordinate's behavior that indicate unsuccessful action and those that indicate poor behavior.
Of the following, a MAJOR disadvantage of this method of performance appraisal is that it
    A. often leads to overly close supervision
    B. results in competition among those subordinates being evaluated
    C. tends to result in superficial judgments
    D. lacks objectivity for evaluating performance

6. Assume that you are a supervisor and have observed the performance of an employee during a period of time. You have concluded that his performance needs improvement.
In order to improve his performance, it would, therefore, be BEST for you to
    A. note your findings in the employee's personnel folder so that his behavior is a matter of record
    B. report the findings to the personnel officer so he can take prompt action
    C. schedule a problem-solving conference with the employee
    D. recommend his transfer to simpler duties

7. When an employee's absences or latenesses seem to be nearing excessiveness, the supervisor should speak with him to find out what the problem is.
Of the following, if such a discussion produces no reasonable explanation, the discussion usually BEST serves to
    A. affirm clearly the supervisor's adherence to proper policy
    B. alert other employees that such behavior is unacceptable
    C. demonstrate that the supervisor truly represents higher management
    D. notify the employee that his behavior is being observed and evaluated

8. Assume that an employee willfully and recklessly violates an important agency regulation. The nature of the violation is of such magnitude that it demands immediate action, but the facts of the case are not entirely clear. Further, assume that the supervisor is free to make any of the following recommendations.
The MOST appropriate action for the supervisor to take is to recommend that the employee be
    A. discharged   B. suspended
    C. forced to resign   D. transferred

9. Although employees' titles may be identical, each position in that title may be considerably different.
Of the following, a supervisor should carefully assign each employee to a specific position based PRIMARILY on the employee's
    A. capability   B. experience   C. education   D. seniority

10. The one of the following situations where it is MOST appropriate to transfer an employee to a similar assignment is one in which the employee
    A. lacks motivation and interest
    B. experiences a personality conflict with his supervisor
    C. is negligent in the performance of his duties
    D. lacks capacity or ability to perform assigned tasks

11. The one of the following which is LEAST likely to be affected by improvements in the morale of personnel is employee
    A. skill
    B. absenteeism
    C. turnover
    D. job satisfaction

12. The one of the following situations in which it is LEAST appropriate for a supervisor to delegate authority to subordinates is where the supervisor
    A. lacks confidence in his own abilities to perform certain work
    B. is overburdened and cannot handle all his responsibilities
    C. refers all disciplinary problems to his subordinate
    D. has to deal with an emergency or crisis

13. Assume that it has come to your attention that two of your subordinates have shouted at each other and have almost engaged in a fist fight. Luckily, they were separated by some of the other employees.
    Of the following, your BEST immediate course of action would generally be to
    A. reprimand the senior of the two subordinates since he should have known better
    B. hear the story from both employees and any witnesses and then take needed disciplinary action
    C. ignore the matter since nobody was physically hurt
    D. immediately suspend and fine both employees pending a departmental hearing

14. You have been delegating some of your authority to one of your subordinates because of his leadership potential.
    Which of the following actions is LEAST conducive to the growth and development of this individual for a supervisory position?
    A. Use praise only when it will be effective
    B. Give very detailed instructions and supervise the employee closely to be sure that the instructions ae followed precisely
    C. Let the subordinate proceed with his planned course of action even if mistakes, within a permissible range, are made
    D. Intervene on behalf of the subordinate whenever an assignment becomes difficult for him

15. A rumor has been spreading in your department concerning the possibility of layoffs due to decreased revenues.
    As a supervisor, you should GENERALLY
    A. deny the rumor, whether it is true or false, in order to keep morale from declining

4 (#2)

    B. inform the men to the best of your knowledge about this situation and keep them advised of any new information
    C. tell the men to forget about the rumor and concentrate on increasing their productivity
    D. ignore the rumor since it is not authorized information

16. Within an organization, every supervisor should know to whom he reports and who reports to him.
The one of the following which is achieved by use of such structured relationships is
    A. unity of command
    B. confidentiality
    C. esprit de corps
    D. promotion opportunities

16.____

17. Almost every afternoon, one of your employees comes back from his break ten minutes late without giving you any explanation.
Which of the following actions should you take FIRST in this situation?
    A. Assign the employee to a different type of work and observe whether his behavior changes
    B. Give the employee extra work to do so that he will have to return on time
    C. Ask the employee for an explanation for his lateness
    D. Tell the employee he is jeopardizing the break for everyone

17.____

18. When giving instructions to your employees in a group, which one of the following should you make certain to do?
    A. Speak in a casual, off-hand manner
    B. Assume that your employees fully understand the instructions
    C. Write out your instructions beforehand and read them to the employees
    D. Tell exactly who is to do what

18.____

19. A fist fight develops between two men under your supervision.
The MOST advisable course of action for you to take FIRST is to
    A. call the police
    B. have the other workers pull them apart
    C. order them to stop
    D. step between the two men

19.____

20. You have assigned some difficult and unusual work to one of your most experienced and competent subordinates.
If you notice that he is doing the work incorrectly, you should
    A. assign the work to another employee
    B. reprimand him in private
    C. show him immediately how the work should be done
    D. wait until the job is completed and then correct his errors

20.____

KEY (CORRECT ANSWERS)

1. D
2. D
3. D
4. B
5. A

6. C
7. D
8. B
9. A
10. B

11. A
12. C
13. B
14. B
15. B

16. A
17. C
18. D
19. C
20. C

PREPARING WRITTEN MATERIAL

PARAGRAPH REARRANGEMENT
COMMENTARY

The sentences that follow are in scrambled order. You are to rearrange them in proper order and indicate the letter choice containing the correct answer at the space at the right.

Each group of sentences in this section is actually a paragraph presented in scrambled order. Each sentence in the group has a place in that paragraph; no sentence is to be left out. You are to read each group of sentences and decide upon the best order in which to put the sentences so as to form a well-organized paragraph.

The questions in this section measure the ability to solve a problem when all the facts relevant to its solution are not given.

More specifically, certain positions of responsibility and authority require the employee to discover connection between events sometimes, apparently, unrelated. In order to do this, the employee will find it necessary to correctly infer that unspecified events have probably occurred or are likely to occur. This ability becomes especially important when action must be taken on incomplete information.

Accordingly, these questions require competitors to choose among several suggested alternatives, each of which presents a different sequential arrangement of the events. Competitors must choose the MOST logical of the suggested sequences.

In order to do so, they may be required to draw on general knowledge to infer missing concepts or events that are essential to sequencing the given events. Competitors should be careful to infer only what is essential to the sequence. The plausibility of the wrong alternatives will always require the inclusion of unlikely events or of additional chains of events which are NOT essential to sequencing the given events.

It's very important to remember that you are looking for the best of the four possible choices, and that the best choice of all may not even be one of the answers you're given to choose from.

There is no one right way to solve these problems. Many people have found it helpful to first write out the order of the sentences, as they would have arranged them, on their scrap paper before looking at the possible answers. If their optimum answer is there, this can save them some time. If it isn't, this method can still give insight into solving the problem. Others find it most helpful to just go through each of the possible choices, contrasting each as they go along. You should use whatever method feels comfortable and works for you.

While most of these types of questions are not that difficult, we've added a higher percentage of the difficult type, just to give you more practice. Usually there are only one or two questions on this section that contain such subtle distinctions that you're unable to answer confidently. And you then may find yourself stuck deciding between two possible choices, neither of which you're sure about.

EXAMINATION SECTION
TEST 1

DIRECTIONS: The sentences that follow are in scrambled order. You are to rearrange them in proper order and indicate the letter choice containing the correct answer. *PRINT THE LETTER OF THE CORRECT ANSWER IN THE SPACE AT THE RIGHT.*

1. Below are four statements labeled W, X, Y and Z. 1.____
    W. He was a strict and fanatic drillmaster.
    X. The word is always used in a derogatory sense and generally shows resentment and anger on the part of the user.
    Y. It is from the name of this Frenchman that we derive our English word, martinet.
    Z. Jean Martinet was the Inspector-General of Infantry during the reign of King Louis XIV.
    The PROPER order in which these sentences should be placed in a paragraph is:
       A. X, Z, W, Y   B. X, Z, Y, W   C. Z, W, Y, X   D. Z, Y, W, X

2. In the following paragraph, the sentences, which are numbered, have been jumbled. 2.____
    I. Since then it has undergone changes.
    II. It was incorporated in 1955 under the laws of the State of New York.
    III. Its primary purposes, a cleaner city, has, however, remained the same.
    IV. The Citizens Committee works in cooperation with the Mayor's Inter-departmental Committee for a Clean City. 3.____
    The order in which these sentences should be arranged to form a well-organized paragraph is:
       A. II, IV, I, III   B. III, IV, I, II   C. IV, II, I, III   D. IV, III, II, I

Questions 3-5.

DIRECTIONS: The sentences listed below are part of a meaningful paragraph but they are not given in their proper order. You are to decide what would be the BEST order in which to put the sentences so as to form a well-organized paragraph. Each sentence has a place in the paragraph; there are no extra sentences. You are then to answer Questions 3 through 5 inclusive on the basis of your rearrangements of these scrambled sentences into a properly organized paragraph.

In 1887 some insurance companies organized an Inspection Department to advise their clients on all phases of fire prevention and protection. Probably this has been due to the smaller annual fire losses in Great Britain than in the United States. It tests various fire prevention devices and appliances and determines manufacturing hazards and their safeguards. Fire research began earlier in the United States and is more advanced than in Great Britain. Later they established a laboratory specializing in electrical, mechanical, hydraulic, and chemical fields.

2 (#1)

3. When the five sentences are arranged in proper order, the paragraph starts with the sentence which begins
    A. "In 1887..."   B. "Probably this..."   C. "It tests..."
    D. "Fire research..."   E. "Later they..."

3._____

4. In the last sentence listed above, "they" refers to
    A. the insurance companies   B. the United States and Great Britain
    C. the Inspection Department   D. clients
    E. technicians

4._____

5. When the above paragraph is properly arranged, it ends with the words
    A. "...and protection."   B. "...the United States."
    C. "...their safeguards."   D. "...in Great Britain."
    E. "...chemical fields."

5._____

KEY (CORRECT ANSWERS)

1. C
2. C
3. D
4. A
5. C

TEST 2

DIRECTIONS: In each of the questions numbered I through V, several sentences are given. For each question, choose as your answer the group of number that represents the MOST logical order of these sentences if they were arranged in paragraph form. *PRINT THE LETTER OF THE CORRECT ANSWER IN THE SPACE AT THE RIGHT.*

1. I. It is established when one shows that the landlord has prevented the tenant's enjoyment of his interest in the property leased.
    II. Constructive eviction is the result of a breach of the covenant of quiet enjoyment implied in all leases.
    III. In some parts of the United States, it is not complete until the tenant vacates within a reasonable time.
    IV. Generally, the acts must be of such serious and permanent character as to deny the tenant the enjoyment of his possessing rights.
    V. In this event, upon abandonment of the premises, the tenant's liability for that ceases.
    The CORRECT answer is:
    A. II, I, IV, III, V
    B. V, II, III, I, IV
    C. IV, III, I, II, V
    D. I, III, V, IV, II

    1.____

2. I. The powerlessness before private and public authorities that is the typical experience of the slum tenant is reminiscent of the situation of blue-collar workers all through the nineteenth century.
    II. Similarly, in recent years, this chapter of history has been reopened by anti-poverty groups which have attempted to organize slum tenants to enable them to bargain collectively with their landlords about the conditions of their tenancies.
    III. It is familiar history that many of the worker remedied their condition by joining together and presenting their demands collectively.
    IV. Like the workers, tenants are forced by the conditions of modern life into substantial dependence on these who possess great political aid and economic power.
    V. What's more, the very fact of dependence coupled with an absence of education and self-confidence makes them hesitant and unable to stand up for what they need from those in power.
    The CORRECT answer is:
    A. V, IV, I, II, III
    B. II, III, I, V, IV
    C. III, I, V, IV, II
    D. I, IV, V, III, II

    2.____

3. I. A railroad, for example, when not acting as a common carrier may contract away responsibility for its own negligence.
    II. As to a landlord, however, no decision has been found relating to the legal effect of a clause shifting the statutory duty of repair to the tenant.
    III. The courts have not passed on the validity of clauses relieving the landlord of this duty and liability.
    IV. They have, however, upheld the validity of exculpatory clauses in other types of contracts.

    3.____

V. Housing regulations impose a duty upon the landlord to maintain leased premises in safe condition.
VI. As another example, a bailee may limit his liability except for gross negligence, willful acts, or fraud.

The CORRECT answer is:
A. II, I, VI, IV, III, V
B. I, III, IV, V, VI, II
C. III, V, I, IV, II, VI
D. V, III, IV, I, VI, II

4.
I. Since there are only samples in the building, retail or consumer sales are generally eschewed by mart occupants, and in some instances, rigid controls are maintained to limit entrance to the mart only to those persons engaged in retailing.
II. Since World War I, in many larger cities, there has developed a new type of property, called the mart building.
III. It can, therefore, be used by wholesalers and jobbers for the display of sample merchandise.
IV. This type of building is most frequently a multi-storied, finished interior property which is a cross between a retail arcade and a loft building.
V. This limitation enables the mart occupants to ship the orders from another location after the retailer or dealer makes his selection from the samples.

The CORRECT answer is:
A. II, IV, III, I, V
B. IV, III, V, I, II
C. I, III, II, IV, V
D. I, IV, II, III, V

5.
I. In general, staff-line friction reduces the distinctive contribution of staff personnel.
II. The conflicts, however, introduce an uncontrolled element into the managerial system.
III. On the other hand, the natural resistance of the line to staff innovations probably usefully restrains over-eager efforts to apply untested procedures on a large scale.
IV. Under such conditions, it is difficult to know when valuable ideas are being sacrificed.
V. The relatively weak position of staff, requiring accommodation to the line, tends to restrict their ability to engage in free, experimental innovation.

The CORRECT answer is:
A. IV, II, III, I, V
B. I, V, III, II, IV
C. V, III, I, II, IV
D. II, I, IV, V, III

KEY (CORRECT ANSWERS)

1. A
2. D
3. D
4. A
5. B

TEST 3

DIRECTIONS: Questions 1 through 4 consist of six sentences which can be arranged in a logical sequence. For each question, select the choice which places the numbered sentences in the MOST logical sequent. *PRINT THE LETTER OF THE CORRECT ANSWER IN THE SPACE AT THE RIGHT.*

1. I. The burden of proof as to each issue is determined before trial and remains upon the same party throughout the trial.
    II. The jury is at liberty to believe one witness' testimony as against a number of contradictory witnesses.
    III. In a civil case, the party bearing the burden of proof is required to prove his contention by a fair preponderance of the evidence.
    IV. However, it must be noted that a fair preponderance of evidence does not necessarily mean a greater number of witnesses.
    V. The burden of proof is the burden which rests upon one of the parties to an action to persuade the trier of the facts, generally the jury, that a proposition he asserts is true.
    VI. If the evidence is equally balanced, or if it leaves the jury in such doubt as to be unable to decide the controversy either way, judgment must be given against the party upon whom the burden of proof rests.
    The CORRECT answer is:
    A. III, II, V, IV, I, VI
    B. I, II, VI, V, III, IV
    C. III, IV, V, I, II, VI
    D. V, I, III, VI, IV, II

    1.____

2. I. If a parent is without assets and is unemployed, he cannot be convicted of the crime of non-support of a child.
    II. The term "sufficient ability" has been held to mean sufficient financial ability.
    III. It does not matter if his unemployment is by choice or unavoidable circumstances.
    IV. If he fails to take any steps at all, he may be liable to prosecution for endangering the welfare of a child.
    V. Under the penal law, a parent is responsible for the support of his minor child only if the parent is "of sufficient ability."
    VI. An indigent parent may meet his obligation by borrowing money or by seeking aid under the provisions of the Social Welfare Law.
    The CORRECT answer is:
    A. VI, I, V, III, II, IV
    B. I, III, V, II, IV, VI
    C. V, II, I, III, VI, IV
    D. I, VI, IV, V, II, III

    2.____

3. I. Consider, for example, the case of a rabble rouser who urges a group of twenty people to go out and break the windows of a nearby factory.
    II. Therefore, the law fills the indicated gap with the crime of inciting to riot.
    III. A person is considered guilty of inciting to riot when he urges ten or more persons to engage in tumultuous and violent conduct of a kind likely to create public alarm.
    IV. However, if he has not obtained the cooperation of at least four people, he cannot be charged with unlawful assembly.

    3.____

99

V. The charge of inciting to riot was added to the law to cover types of conduct which cannot be classified as either the crime of "riot" or the crime of "unlawful assembly."
VI. If he acquires the acquiescence of at least four of them, he is guilty of unlawful assembly even if the project does not materialize.

The CORRECT answer is:
A. III, V, I, VI, IV, II
B. V, I, IV, VI, II, III
C. III, IV, I, V, II, VI
D. V, I, IV, VI, III, II

4. I. If, however, the rebuttal evidence presents an issue of credibility, it is for the jury to determine whether the presumption has, in fact, been destroyed.
II. Once sufficient evidence to the contrary is introduced, the presumption disappears from the trial.
III. The effect of a presumption is to place the burden upon the adversary to come forward with evidence to rebut the presumption.
IV. When a presumption is overcome and ceases to exist in the case, the fact or facts which gave rise to the presumption still remain.
V. Whether a presumption has been overcome is ordinarily a question for the court.
VI. Such information may furnish a basis for a logical inference.

The CORRECT answer is:
A. IV, VI, II, V, I, III
B. III, II, V, I, IV, VI
C. V, III, VI, IV, II, I
D. V, IV, I, II, VI, III

KEY (CORRECT ANSWERS)

1. D
2. C
3. A
4. B

PREPARING WRITTEN MATERIAL
EXAMINATION SECTION
TEST 1

DIRECTIONS: Each of Questions 1 through 5 consists of a sentence which may or may not be an example of good formal English usage. Examine each sentence, considering grammar, punctuation, spelling, capitalization, and awkwardness. Then choose the correct statement about it from the four options below it. If the English usage in the sentence given is better than any of the changes suggested in options B, C, or D, pick option A. (Do not pick an option that will change the meaning of the sentence.) *PRINT THE LETTER OF THE CORRECT ANSWER IN THE SPACE AT THE RIGHT.*

1. I don't know who could possibly of broken it. 1.____
   A. This is an example of good formal English usage.
   B. The word "who" should be replaced by the word "whom."
   C. The word "of" should be replaced by the word "have."
   D. The word "broken" should be replaced by the word "broke."

2. Telephoning is easier than to write. 2.____
   A. This is an example of good formal English usage.
   B. The word "telephoning" should be spelled "telephoneing."
   C. The word "than" should be replaced by the word "then."
   D. The words "to write" should be replaced by the word "writing."

3. The two operators who have been assigned to these consoles are on vacation. 3.____
   A. This is an example of good formal English usage.
   B. A comma should be placed after the word "operators."
   C. The word "who" should be replaced by the word "whom."
   D. The word "are" should be replaced by the word "is."

4. You were suppose to teach me how to operate a plugboard. 4.____
   A. This is an example of good formal English usage.
   B. The word "were" should be replaced by the word "was."
   C. The word "suppose" should be replaced by the word "supposed."
   D. The word "teach" should be replaced by the word "learn."

5. If you had taken my advice; you would have spoken with him. 5.____
   A. This is an example of good formal English usage.
   B. The word "advice" should be spelled "advise."
   C. The words "had taken" should be replaced by the word "take."
   D. The semicolon should be changed to a comma.

KEY (CORRECT ANSWERS)

1. C
2. D
3. A
4. C
5. D

TEST 2

DIRECTIONS: Select the correct answer. *PRINT THE LETTER OF THE CORRECT ANSWER IN THE SPACE AT THE RIGHT.*

1. The one of the following sentences which is MOST acceptable from the viewpoint of correct grammatical usage is:
   A. I do not know which action will have worser results.
   B. He should of known better.
   C. Both the officer on the scene, and his immediate supervisor, is charged with the responsibility.
   D. An officer must have initiative because his supervisor will not always be available to answer questions.

   1.____

2. The one of the following sentences which is MOST acceptable from the viewpoint of correct grammatical usage is:
   A. Of all the officers available, the better one for the job will be picked.
   B. Strict orders were given to all the officers, except he.
   C. Study of the law will enable you to perform your duties more efficiently.
   D. It seems to me that you was wrong in failing to search the two men.

   2.____

3. The one of the following sentences which does NOT contain a misspelled word is:
   A. The duties you will perform are similar to the duties of a patrolman.
   B. Officers must be constantly alert to sieze the initiative.
   C. Officers in this organization are not entitled to special privileges.
   D. Any changes in procedure will be announced publically.

   3.____

4. The one of the following sentences which does NOT contain a misspelled word is:
   A. It will be to your advantage to keep your firearm in good working condition.
   B. There are approximately fourty men on sick leave.
   C. Your first duty will be to pursuade the person to obey the law.
   D. Fires often begin in flameable material kept in lockers.

   4.____

5. The one of the following sentences which does NOT contain a misspelled word is:
   A. Offices are not required to perform technical maintainance.
   B. He violated the regulations on two occasions.
   C. Every employee will be held responable for errors.
   D. This was his nineth absence in a year.

   5.____

KEY (CORRECT ANSWERS)

1. D
2. C
3. C
4. A
5. B

TEST 3

DIRECTIONS: Select the correct answer. *PRINT THE LETTER OF THE CORRECT ANSWER IN THE SPACE AT THE RIGHT.*

1. You are answering a letter that was written on the letterhead of the ABC Company and signed by James H. Wood, Treasurer.
   What is usually considered to be the correct salutation to use in your reply?
   A. Dear ABC Company:
   B. Dear Sirs:
   C. Dear Mr. Wood:
   D. Dear Mr. Treasurer:

   1._____

2. Assume that one of your duties is to handle routine letters of inquiry from the public.
   The one of the following which is usually considered to be MOST desirable in replying to such a letter is a
   A. detailed answer handwritten on the original letter of inquiry
   B. phone call, since you can cover details more easily over the phone than in a letter
   C. short letter giving the specific information requested
   D. long letter discussing all possible aspects of the question raised

   2._____

3. The CHIEF reason for dividing a letter into paragraphs is to
   A. make the message clear to the reader by starting a new paragraph for each new topic
   B. make a short letter occupy as much of the page as possible
   C. keep the reader's attention by providing a pause from time to time
   D. make the letter look neat and businesslike

   3._____

4. Your superior has asked you to send an e-mail from your agency to a government agency in another city. He has written out the message and has indicated the name of the government agency.
   When you dictate the message to your secretary, which of the following items that your superior has NOT mentioned must you be sure to include?
   A. Today's date
   B. The full address of the government agency
   C. A polite opening such as "Dear Sirs"
   D. A final sentence such as "We would appreciate hearing from your agency in reply as soon as is convenient for you"

   4._____

5. The one of the following sentences which is grammatically preferable to the others is:
   A. Our engineers will go over your blueprints so that you may have no problems in construction.
   B. For a long time he had been arguing that we, not he, are to blame for the confusion.
   C. I worked on this automobile for two hours and still cannot find out what is wrong with it.
   D. Accustomed to all kinds of hardships, fatigue seldom bothers veteran policemen.

   5._____

KEY (CORRECT ANSWERS)

1. C
2. C
3. A
4. B
5. A

TEST 4

DIRECTIONS: Select the correct answer. *PRINT THE LETTER OF THE CORRECT ANSWER IN THE SPACE AT THE RIGHT.*

1. Suppose that an applicant for a job as snow laborer presents a letter from a former employer stating: "John Smith has a pleasing manner and never got into an argument with his fellow employees. He was never late or absent." This letter
    A. indicates that with some training Smith will make a good snow gang boss
    B. presents no definite evidence of Smith's ability to do snow work
    C. proves definitely that Smith has never done any snow work before
    D. proves definitely that Smith will do better than average work as a snow laborer

    1.____

2. Suppose you must write a letter to a local organization in your section refusing a request in connection with collection of their refuse.
    You should start the letter by
    A. explaining in detail the consideration you gave the request
    B. praising the organization for its service to the community
    C. quoting the regulation which forbids granting the request
    D. stating your regret that the request cannot be granted

    2.____

3. Suppose a citizen writes in for information as to whether or not he may sweep refuse into the gutter. A Sanitation officer answers as follows:
    Dear Sir:
      No person is permitted to litter, sweep, throw or cast, or direct, suffer or permit any person under his control to litter, sweep, throw or cast any ashes, garbage, paper, dust, or other rubbish or refuse into any public street or place, vacant lot, air shaft, areaway, backyard or court.
                                Very truly yours,
                                John Doe
    This letter is *poorly* written CHIEFLY because
    A. the opening is not indented   B. the thought is not clear
    C. the tone is too formal and cold   D. there are too many commas used

    3.____

4. A section of a disciplinary report written by a Sanitation officer states: "It is requested that subject Sanitation man be advised that his future activities be directed towards reducing his recurrent tardiness else disciplinary action will be initiated which may result in summary discharge."
    This section of the report is *poorly* written MAINLY because
    A. at least one word is misspelled   B. it is not simply expressed
    C. more than one idea is expressed   D. the purpose is not stated

    4.____

5. A section of a disciplinary report written by an officer states: "He comes in late. He takes too much time for lunch. He is lazy. I recommend his services be dispensed with."
    This section of the report is *poorly* written MAINLY because
    A. it ends with a preposition   B. it is not well organized
    C. no supporting facts are stated   D. the sentences are too simple

    5.____

KEY (CORRECT ANSWERS)

1. B
2. D
3. C
4. B
5. C

SUPERVISION STUDY GUIDE

Social science has developed information about groups and leadership in general and supervisor-employee relationships in particular. Since organizational effectiveness is closely linked to the ability of supervisors to direct the activities of employees, these findings are important to executives everywhere.

IS A SUPERVISOR A LEADER?

First-line supervisors are found in all large business and government organizations. They are the men at the base of an organizational hierarchy. Decisions made by the head of the organization reach them through a network of intermediate positions. They are frequently referred to as part of the management team, but their duties seldom seem to support this description.

A supervisor of clerks, tax collectors, meat inspectors, or securities analysts is not charged with budget preparation. He cannot hire or fire the employees in his own unit on his say-so. He does not administer programs which require great planning, coordinating, or decision making.

Then what is he? He is the man who is directly in charge of a group of employees doing productive work for a business or government agency. If the work requires the use of machines, the men he supervises operate them. If the work requires the writing of reports, the men he supervises write them. He is expected to maintain a productive flow of work without creating problems which higher levels of management must solve. But is he a leader?

To carry out a specific part of an agency's mission, management creates a unit, staffs it with a group of employees and designates a supervisor to take charge of them. Management directs what this unit shall do, from time to time changes directions, and often indicates what the group should not do. Management presumably creates status for the supervisor by giving him more pay, a title, and special privileges.

Management asks a supervisor to get his workers to attain organizational goals, including the desired quantity and quality of production. Supposedly, he has authority to enable him to achieve this objective. Management at least assumes that by establishing the status of the supervisor's position, it has created sufficient authority to enable him to achieve these goals—not his goals, nor necessarily the group's, but management's goals.

In addition, supervision includes writing reports, keeping records of membership in a higher-level administrative group, industrial engineering, safety engineering, editorial duties, housekeeping duties, etc. The supervisor as a member of an organizational network, must be responsible to the changing demands of the management above him. At the same time, he must be responsive to the demands of the work group of which he is a member. He is placed in the difficult position of communicating and implementing new decisions, changed programs and revised production quotas for his work group, although he may have had little part in developing them.

It follows, then, that supervision has a special characteristic: achievement of goals, previously set by management, through the efforts of others. It is in this feature of the supervisor's job that we find the role of a leader in the sense of the following definition: *A leader is that person who <u>most</u> effectively influences group activities toward goal setting and goal achievements.*

This definition is broad. It covers both leaders in groups that come together voluntarily and in those brought together through a work assignment in a factory, store, or government agency. In the natural group, the authority necessary to attain goals is determined by the group membership and is granted by them. In the working group, it is apparent that the establishment of a supervisory position creates a predisposition on the part of employees to accept the authority of the occupant of that position. We cannot, however, assume that mere occupation confers authority sufficient to assure the accomplishment of an organization's goals.

Supervision is different, then, from leadership. The supervisor is expected to fulfill the role of leader but without obtaining a grant of authority from the group he supervises. The supervisor is expected to influence the group in the achieving of goals but is often handicapped by having little influence on the organizational process by which goals are set. The supervisor, because he works in an organizational setting, has the burdens of additional organizational duties and restrictions and requirements arising out of the fact that his position is subordinate to a hierarchy of higher-level supervisors. These differences between leadership and supervision are reflected in our definition: *Supervision is basically a leadership role, in a formal organization, which has as its objective the effective influencing of other employees.*

Even though these differences between supervision and leadership exist, a significant finding of experimenters in this field is that supervisors <u>must</u> be leaders to be successful.

The problem is: How can a supervisor exercise leadership in an organizational setting? We might say that the supervisor is expected to be a natural leader in a situation which does not come about naturally. His situation becomes really difficult in an organization which is more eager to make its supervisors into followers rather than leaders.

LEADERSHIP: NATURAL AND ORGANIZATIONAL

Leadership, in its usual sense of *natural* leadership, and supervision are not the same. In some cases, leadership embraces broader powers and functions than supervision; in other cases, supervision embraces more than leadership. This is true both because of the organization and technical aspects of the supervisor's job and because of the relatively freer setting and inherent authority of the natural leader.

The natural leader usually has much more authority and influence than the supervisor. Group members not only follow his command but prefer it that way. The employee, however, can appeal the supervisor's commands to his union or to the supervisor's superior or to the personnel office. These intercessors represent restrictions on the supervisor's power to lead.

The natural leader can gain greater membership involvement in the group's objectives, and he can change the objectives of the group. The supervisor can attempt to gain employee support only for management's objectives; he cannot set other objectives. In these instances leadership is broader than supervision.

The natural leader must depend upon whatever skills are available when seeking to attain objectives. The supervisor is trained in the administrative skills necessary to achieve management's goals. If he does not possess the requisite skills, however, he can call upon management's technicians.

A natural leader can maintain his leadership, in certain groups, merely by satisfying members' need for group affiliation. The supervisor must maintain his leadership by directing and organizing his group to achieve specific organizational goals set for him and his group by management. He must have a technical competence and a kind of coordinating ability which is not needed by many natural leaders.

A natural leader is responsible only to his group which grants him authority. The supervisor is responsible to management, which employs him, and also to the work group of which he is a member. The supervisor has the exceedingly difficult job of reconciling the demands of two groups frequently in conflict. He is often placed in the untenable position of trying to play two antagonistic roles. In the above instance, supervision is broader than leadership.

ORGANIZATIONAL INFLUENCES ON LEADERSHIP

The supervisor is both a product and a prisoner of the organization wherein we find him. The organization which creates the supervisor's position also obstructs, restricts, and channelizes the exercise of his duties. These influences extend beyond prescribed functional relationships to specific supervisory behavior. For example, even in a face-to-face situation involving one of his subordinates, the supervisor's actions are controlled to a great extent by his organization. His behavior must conform to the organization policy on human relations, rules which dictate personnel procedures, specific prohibitions governing conduct, the attitudes of his own superior, etc. He is not a free agent operating within the limits of his work group. His freedom of action is much more circumscribed than is generally admitted. The organizational influences which limit his leadership actions can be classified as structure, prescriptions, and proscriptions.

The organizational structure places each supervisor's position in context with other designated positions. It determines the relationships between his position and specific positions which impinge on his. The structure of the organization designates a certain position to which he looks for orders and information about his work. It gives a particular status to his position within a pattern of statuses from which he perceives that (1) certain positions are on a par, organizationally, with his, (2) other positions are subordinate, and (3) still others are superior.

The organizational structure determines those positions to which he should look for advice and assistance, and those positions to which he should give advice and assistance.

For instance, the organizational structure has predetermined that the supervisor of a clerical processing unit shall report to a supervisory position in a higher echelon. He shall have certain relationships with the supervisors of the work units which transmit work to and receive work from his unit. He shall discuss changes and clarification of procedures with certain staff units, such as organization and methods, cost accounting, and personnel. He shall consult supervisors of units which provide or receive special work assignments.

The organizational structure, however, establishes patterns other than those of the relationships of positions. These are the patterns of responsibility, authority, and expectations.

The supervisor is responsible for certain activities or results; he is presumably invested with the authority to achieve these. His set of authority and responsibility is interwoven with other sets to the end that all goals and functions of the organization are parceled out in small, manageable lots. This, of course, establishes a series of expectations: a single supervisor can perform his particular set of duties only upon the assumption that preceding or contiguous sets of duties have been, or are being carried out. At the same time, he is aware of the expectations of others that he will fulfill his functional role.

The structure of an organization establishes relationships between specified positions and specific expectations for these positions. The fact that these relationships and expectations are established is one thing; whether or not they are met is another.

PRESCRIPTIONS AND PROSCRIPTIONS

But let us return to the organizational influences which act to restrict the supervisor's exercise of leadership. These are the prescriptions and proscriptions generally in effect in all organizations, and those peculiar to a single organization. In brief these are the *thou shalt's* and the *thou shalt not's*.

Organizations not only prescribe certain duties for individual supervisory positions, they also prescribe specific methods and means of carrying out these duties and maintaining management-employee relations. These include rules, regulations, policy, and tradition. It does no good for the supervisor to say, *This seems to be the best way to handle such-and-such,* if the organization has established a routine for dealing with problems. For good or bad, there are rules that state that firings shall be executed in such a manner, accompanied by a certain notification; that training shall be conducted, and in this manner. Proscriptions are merely negative prescriptions; you may not discriminate against any employee because of politics or race; you shall not suspend any employee without following certain procedures and obtaining certain approvals.

Most of these prohibitions and rules apply to the area of interpersonal relations, precisely the area which is now arousing most interest on the part of administrators and managers. We have become concerned about the contrast between formally prescribed relationships and interpersonal relationships, and this brings us to the often discussed informal organization.

FORMAL AND INFORMAL ORGANIZATIONS

As we well know, the functions and activities of any organization are broken down into individual units of work called positions. Administrators must establish a pattern which will link these positions to each other and relate them to a system of authority and responsibility. Man-to-man are spelled out as plainly as possible for all to understand. Managers, then, build an official structure which we call the formal organization.

In these same organizations, employees react individually and in groups to institutionally determined roles. John, a worker, rides in the same carpool as Joe, a foreman. An unplanned communication develops. Harry, a machinist knows more about high-speed machining than his foreman or anyone else in his shop. An unofficial tool boss comes into being. Mary, who fought with Jane, is promoted over her. Jane now gives Mary's directions. A planned relationship fails to develop. The employees have built a structure which we call the informal organization.

Formal organization is a system of management-prescribed relations between positions in an organization.

Informal organization is a network of unofficial relations between people in an organization.

These definitions might lead us to the absurd conclusion that positions carry out formal activities and that employe4es spend their time in unofficial activities. We must recognize that organizational activities are in all cases carried out by people. The formal structure provides a needed framework within which interpersonal relations occur. What we call informal organization is the complex of normal, natural relations among employees. These personal relationships may be negative or positive. That is, they may impede or aid the achievement of organizational goals. For example, friendship between two supervisors greatly increases the probability of good cooperation and coordination between their sections. On the other hand, *buck passing* nullifies the formal structure by failure to meet a prescribed and expected responsibility.

It is improbable that an ideal organization exists where all activities are carried out in strict conformity to a formally prescribed pattern of functional roles. Informal organization arises because of the incompleteness and ambiguities in the network of formally prescribed relationships, or in response to the needs or inadequacies of supervisors or managers who hold prescribed functional roles in an organization. Many of these relationships are not prescribed by the organizational pattern; many cannot be prescribed; many should not be prescribed.

Management faces the problem of keeping the informal organization in harmony with the mission of the agency. One way to do this is to make sure that all employees have a clear understanding of and are sympathetic with that mission. The issuance of organizational charts, procedural manuals, and functional descriptions of the work to be done by divisions and sections helps communicate management's plans and goals. Issuances alone, of course, cannot do the whole job. They should be accompanied by oral discussion and explanation. Management must ensure that there is mutual understanding and acceptance of charts and procedures. More important is that management acquaint itself with the attitudes, activities, and peculiar brands of logic which govern the informal organization. Only through this type of knowledge can they and supervisors keep informal goals consistent with the agency mission.

SUPERVISION STATUS AND FUNCTIONAL ROLE

A well-established supervisor is respected by the employees who work with him. They defer to his wishes. It is clear that a superior-subordinate relationship has been established. That is, status of the supervisor has been established in relation to other employees of the same work group. This same supervisor gains the respect of employees when he behaves in as certain manner. He will be expected, generally, to follow the customs of the group in such matters as dress, recreation, and manner of speaking. The group has a set of expectations as to his behavior. His position is a functional role which carries with it a collection of rights and obligations.

The position of supervisor usually has a status distinct from the individual who occupies it: it is much like a position description which exists whether or not there is an incumbent. The status of a supervisory position is valued higher than that of an employee position both because of the functional role of leadership which is assigned to it and because of the status symbols of titles, rights, and privileges which go with it.

Social ranking, or status, is not simple because it involves both the position and the man. An individual may be ranked higher than others because of his education, social background, perceived leadership ability, or conformity to group customs and ideals. If such a man is ranked higher by the members of a work group than their supervisor, the supervisor's effectiveness may be seriously undermined.

If the organization does not build and reinforce a supervisor's status, his position can be undermined in a different way. This will happen when managers go around rather than through the supervisor or designate him as a straw boss, acting boss, or otherwise not a real boss.

Let us clarify this last point. A role, and corresponding status, establishes a set of expectations. Employees expect their supervisor to do certain things and to act in certain ways. They are prepared to respond to that expected behavior. When the supervisor's behavior does not conform to their expectations, they are surprised, confused, and ill-at-ease. It becomes necessary for them to resolve their confusion, if they can. They might do this by turning to one of their own members for leadership. If the confusion continues, or their attempted solutions are not satisfactory, they will probably become a poorly motivated, non-cohesive group which cannot function very well.

COMMUNICATION AND THE SUPERVISOR

In a recent survey, railroad workers reported that they rarely look to their supervisor for information about the company. This is startling, at least to us, because we ordinarily think of the supervisor as the link between management and worker. We expect the supervisor to be the prime source of information about the company. Actually, the railroad workers listed the supervisor next to last in the o5rder of their sources of information. Most surprising of all, the supervisors, themselves, stated that rumor and unofficial contacts were their principal sources of information. Here we see one of the reasons why supervisors may not be as effective as management desires.

The supervisor is not only being bypassed by his work group, he is being ignored, and his position weakened, by the very organization which is holding him responsible for the activities of his workers. If he is management's representative to the employee, then management has an obligation to keep him informed of its activities. This is necessary if he is to carry out his functions efficiently and maintain his leadership in the work group. The supervisor is expected to be a source of information; when he is not, his status is not clear, and employees are dissatisfied because he has not lived up to expectations.

By providing information to the supervisor to pass along to employees, we can strengthen his position as leader of the group, and increase satisfaction and cohesion within the group. Because he has more information than the other members, receives information sooner, and passes it along at the proper times, members turn to him as a source and also provide him with information in the hope of receiving some in return. From this, we can see an increase in group cohesiveness because:

- Employees are bound closer to their supervisor because he is *in the know*.
- There is less need to go outside the group for answers
- Employees will more quickly turn to the supervisor for enlightenment

The fact that he has the answers will also enhance the supervisor's standing in the eyes of his men. This increased status will serve to bolster his authority and control of the group and will probably result in improved morale and productivity.

The foregoing, of course, does not mean that all management information should be given out. There are obviously certain policy determinations and discussions which need not or cannot be transmitted to all supervisors. However, the supervisor must be kept as fully informed as possible so that he can answer questions when asked and can allay needless fears and anxieties. Further, the supervisor has the responsibility of encouraging employee questions and submissions of information. He must be able to present information to employees so that it is clearly understood and accepted. His attitude and manner should make it clear that he believes in what he is saying, that the information is necessary or desirable to the group, and that he is prepared to act on the basis of the information.

SUPERVISION AND JOB PERFORMANCE

The productivity of work groups is a product; employees' efforts are multiplied by the supervision they receive. Many investigators have analyzed this relationship and have discovered elements of supervision which differentiate high and low production groups. These researchers have identified certain types of supervisory practices which they classify as *employee-centered* and other types which they classify as *production centered*.

The difference between these two kinds of supervision lies not in specific practices but in the approach or orientation to supervision. The employee-centered supervisor directs most of his efforts toward increasing employee motivation. He is concerned more with realizing the potential energy of persons than with administrative and technological methods of increasing efficiency and productivity. He is the man who finds ways of causing employees to want to work harder with the same tools. These supervisors emphasize the personal relations between their employees and themselves.

Now, obviously, these pictures are overdrawn. No one supervisor has all the virtues of the ideal type of employee-centered supervisor. And, fortunately, no one supervisor has all the bad traits found in many production-centered supervisors. We should remember that the various practices that researchers have fond which distinguish these two kinds of supervision represent the many practices and methods of supervisors of all gradations between these extremes. We should be careful, too, of the implications of the labels attached to the two types. For instance, being production-centered is not necessarily bad, since the principal responsibility of any supervisor is maintaining the production level that is expected of his work group. Being employee-centered may not necessarily be good, if the only result is a happy, chuckling crew of loafers. To return to the researchers' findings, employee-centered supervisors:

- Recommend promotions, transfers, pay increases
- Inform men about what is happening in the company
- Keep men posted on how well they are doing
- Hear complaints and grievances sympathetically
- Speak up for subordinates

Production-centered supervisors, on the other hand, don't do those things. They check on employees more frequently, give more detailed and frequent instructions, don't give reasons for changes, and are more punitive when mistakes are made. Employee-centered supervisors were reported to contribute to high morale and high production, whereas production-centered supervision was associated with lower morale and less production.

More recent findings, however, show that the relationship between supervision and productivity is not this simple. Investigators now report that high production is more frequently associated with supervisory practices which combine employee-centered behavior with concern for production. (This concern is not the same, however, as anxiety about production, which is the hallmark of our production-centered supervisor.) Let us examine these apparently contradictory findings and the premises from which they are derived.

SUPERVISION AND MORALE

Why do supervisory activities cause high or low production? As the name implies, the activities of the employee-centered supervisor tend to relate him more closely and satisfactorily to his workers. The production-centered supervisor's practices tend to separate him from his group and to foster antagonism. An analysis of this difference may answer our question.

Earlier, we pointed out that the supervisor is a type of leader and that leadership is intimately related to the group in which it occurs We discover, now, that an employee-centered supervisor's primary activities are concerned with both his leadership and his group membership. Such a supervisor is a member of a group and occupies a leadership role in that group.

These facts are sometimes obscured when we speak of the supervisor as management's representative, or as the organizational link between management and the employee, or as the end of the chain of command. If we really want to understand what it is we expect of the supervisor, we must remember that he is the designated leader of a group of employees to whom he is bound by interaction and interdependence.

Most of his actions are aimed, consciously or unconsciously, at strengthening membership ties in the group. This includes both making members more conscious that he is a member of their group) and causing members to identify themselves more closely with the group. These ends are accomplished by:

- making the group more attractive to the worker: they find satisfaction of their needs for recognition, friendship, enjoyable work, etc.;
- maintaining open communication: employees can express their views and obtain information about the organization
- giving assistance: members can seek advice on personal problems as well as their work; and
- acting as a buffer between the group and management: he speaks up for his men and explains the reasons for management's decisions.

Such actions both strengthen group cohesiveness and solidarity and affirm the supervisor's leadership position in the group.

DEFINING MORALE

This brings us back to a point mentioned earlier. We had said that employee-centered supervisors contribute to high morale as well as to high production. But how can we explain units which have low morale and high productivity, or vice versa? Usually production and morale are considered separately, partly because they are measured against different criteria and partly because, in some instances, they seem to be independent of each other.

Some of this difficulty may stem from confusion over definitions of morale. Morale has been defined as, or measured by, absences from work, satisfaction with job or company, dissension among members of work groups, productivity, apathy or lack of interest, readiness to help others, and a general aura of happiness as rated by observers. Some of these criteria of morale are not subject to the influence of the supervisor, and some of them are not clearly related to productivity. Definitions like these invite findings of low morale coupled with high production.

Both productivity and morale can be influenced by environmental factors not under the control of group members or supervisors. Such things as plant layout, organizational structure and goals, lighting, ventilation, communications, and management planning may have an adverse or desirable effect.

We might resolve the dilemma by defining morale on the basis of our understanding of the supervisor as leader of a group; morale is the degree of satisfaction of group members with their leadership. In this light, the supervisor's employee-centered activities bear a clear relation to morale. His efforts to increase employee identification with the group and to strengthen his leadership lead to greater satisfaction with that leadership. By increasing group cohesiveness and by demonstrating that his influence and power can aid the group, he is able to enhance his leadership status and afford satisfaction to the group.

SUPERVISION, PRODUCTION, AND MORALE

There are factors within the organization itself which determine whether increased production is possible:

- Are production goals expressed in terms understandable to employees and are they realistic?
- Do supervisors responsible for production respect the agency mission and production goals?
- If employees do not know how to do the job well, does management provide a trainer—often the supervisor—who can teach efficient work methods?

There are other factors within the work group which determine whether increased production will be attained:

- Is leadership present which can bring about the desired level of production?
- Are production goals accepted by employees as reasonable and attainable?
- If group effort is involved, are members able to coordinate their efforts?

Research findings confirm the view that an employee-centered supervisor can achieve higher morale than a production-centered supervisor. Managers may well ask what is the relationship between this and production.

Supervision is production-oriented to the extent that it focuses attention on achieving organizational goals, and plans and devises methods for attaining them; it is employee-centered to the extent that it focuses attention on employee attitudes toward those goals, and plans and works toward maintenance of employee satisfaction.

High productivity and low morale result when a supervisor plans and organizes work efficiently but cannot achieve high membership satisfaction. Low production and high morale result when a supervisor, though keeping members satisfied with his leadership, either has not gained acceptance of organizational goals or does not have the technical competence to achieve them.

The relationship between supervision, morale, and productivity is an interdependent one, with the supervisor playing an integral role due to his ability to influence productivity and morale independently of each other.

A supervisor who can plan his work well has good technical knowledge, and who can install better production methods can raise production without necessarily increasing group satisfaction. On the other hand, a supervisor who can motivate his employees and keep them satisfied with his leadership can gain high production in spite of technical difficulties and environmental obstacles.

CLIMATE AND SUPERVISION

Climate, the intangible environment of an organization made up of attitudes, beliefs, and traditions, plays a large part in morale, productivity, and supervision. Usually when we speak of climate and its relationship to morale and productivity, we talk about the merits of *democratic* versus *authoritarian* climate. Employees seem to produce more and have higher morale in a democratic climate, whereas in an authoritarian climate, the reverse seems to be true or so the researchers tell us. We would do well to determine what these terms mean to supervision.

Perhaps most of our difficulty in understanding and applying these concepts comes from our emotional reactions to the words themselves. For example, authoritarian climate is usually painted as the very blackest kind of dictatorship. This is not surprising, because we are usually expected to believe that it is invariably bad. Conversely, democratic climate is drawn to make the driven snow look impure by comparison.

Now these descriptions are most probably true when we talk about our political processes, or town meetings, or freedom of speech. However, the same labels have been used by social scientists in other contexts and have also been applied to government and business organizations, without it, it seems, any recognition that the meanings and their social values may have changed somewhat

For example, these labels were used in experiments conducted in an informal classroom setting using 11-year-old boys as subjects. The descriptive labels applied to the climate of the setting as well as the type of leadership practiced. When these labels were transferred to a management setting, it seems that many presumed that they principally meant the king of leadership rather than climate. We can see that there is a great difference between the experimental and management settings and that leadership practices for one might be inappropriate for the other.

It is doubtful that formal work organizations can be anything but authoritarian, in that goals are set by management and a hierarchy exists through which decisions and orders from the top are transmitted downward. Organizations are authoritarian by structure and need; direction and control are placed in the hands of a few in order to gain fast and efficient decision making. Now this does not mean to describe a dictatorship. It is merely the recognition of the fact that direction of organizational affairs comes from above. It should be noted that leadership in some natural groups is, in this sense, authoritarian.

Granting that formal organizations have this kind of authoritarian leadership, can there be a democratic climate? Certainly there can be, but we would want to define and delimit this term. A more realistic meaning of democratic climate in organizations is the use of permissive and participatory methods in management-employee relations. That is, a mutual exchange of information and explanation with the granting of individual freedom within certain restricted and defined limits. However, it is not our purpose to debate the merits of authoritarianism versus democracy. We recognize that within the small work group there is a need for freedom from constraint and an increase in participation in order to achieve organizational goals within the framework of the organizational movement.

Another aspect of climate is best expressed by this familiar, and true, saying: actions speak louder than words. Of particular concern to us is this effect of management climate on the behavior of supervisors, particularly in employee-centered activities.

There have been reports of disappointment with efforts to make supervisors ore employee-centered. Managers state that, since research has shown ways of improving human relations, supervisors should begin to practice these methods. Usually a training course in human relations is established; and supervisors are given this training. Managers then sit back and wait for the expected improvements, only to find that there are none.

If we wish to produce changes in the supervisor's behavior, the climate must be made appropriate and rewarding to the changed behavior. This means that top-level attitudes and behavior cannot deny or contradict the change we are attempting to effect. Basic changes in organizational behavior cannot be made with any permanence, unless we provide an environment that is receptive to the changes and rewards those persons who do change.

IMPROVING SUPERVISION

Anyone who has read this far might expect to find *A Dozen Rules for Dealing With Employees* or *29 Steps to Supervisory Success*. We will not provide such a list.

Simple rules suffer from their simplicity. They ignore the complexities of human behavior. Reliance upon rules may cause supervisors to concentrate on superficial aspects of their relations with employees. It may preclude genuine understanding.

The supervisor who relies on a list of rules tends to think of people in mechanistic terms. In a certain situation, he uses *Rule No. 3*. Employees are not treated as thinking and feeling persons, but rather as figures in a formula: Rule 3 applied to employee X = Production.

Employees usually recognize mechanical manipulation and become dissatisfied and resentful. They lose faith in, and respect for, their supervisor, and this may be reflected in lower morale and productivity.

We do not mean that supervisors must become social science experts if they wish to improve. Reports of current research indicate that there are two major parts of their job which can be strengthened through self-improvement: (1) Work planning, including technical skills, and (2) motivation of employees.

The most effective supervisors combine excellence in the administrative and technical aspects of their work with friendly and considerate personal relations with their employees.

CRITICAL PERSONAL RELATIONS

Later in this chapter we shall talk about administrative aspects of supervision, but first let us comment on *friendly and considerate personal relations*. We have discussed this subject throughout the preceding chapters, but we want to review some of the critical supervisory influences on personal relations.

Closeness of Supervision: The closeness of supervision has an important effect on productivity and morale. Mann and Dent found that supervisors of low-producing units supervise very closely, while high-producing supervisors exercise only general supervision. It was found that the low-producing supervisors:

- check on employees more frequently
- give more detailed and frequent instructions
- limit employee's freedom to do job in own way

Workers who felt less closely supervised reported that they were better satisfied with their jobs and the company. We should note that the manner or attitude of the supervisor has an important bearing on whether employees perceive supervision as being close or general.

These findings are another way of saying that supervision does not mean standing over the employee and telling him what to do and when and how to do it. The more effective supervisor tells his employees what is required, giving general instructions.

COMMUNICATION

Supervisors of high-production units consider communication as one of the most important aspects of their job. Effective communication is used by these supervisors to achieve better interpersonal relations and improved employee motivation. Low-production supervisors do not rate communications as highly important.

High-producing supervisors find that an important aid to more effective communication is listening. They are ready to listen to both personal problems or interests and questions about the work. This does not mean that they are *nosey* or meddle in their employees' personal lives, but rather that they show a willingness to listen, and do listen, if their employees wish to discuss problems.

These supervisors inform employees about forthcoming changes in work; they discuss agency policy with employees; and they make sure that each employee knows how well he is doing. What these supervisors do is use two-way communication effectively. Unless the supervisor freely imparts information, he will not receive information in return.

Attitudes and perception are frequently affected by communication or the lack of it. Research surveys reveal that many supervisors are not aware of their employees' attitudes, nor do they know what personal reactions their supervision arouses. Through frank discussion with employees, they have been surprised to discover employee beliefs about which they were ignorant. Discussion sometimes reveals that the supervisor and his employees have totally different impressions about the same event. The supervisor should be constantly on the alert for misconceptions about his words and deeds. He must remember that, although his actions are perfectly clear to himself, they may be, and frequently are, viewed differently by employees.

Failure to communicate information results in misconceptions and false assumptions. What you say and how you say it will strongly affect your employees' attitudes and perceptions. By giving them available information, you can prevent misconceptions; by discussion, you may be able to change attitudes; by questioning, you can discover what the perceptions and assumptions really are. And it need hardly be added that actions should conform very closely to words.

If we were to attempt to reduce the above discussion on communication to rules, we would have a long list which would be based on one cardinal principle: Don't make assumptions!

- Don't assume that your employees know; tell them.
- Don't assume that you know how they feel; find out.
- Don't assume that they understand; clarify.

20 SUPERVISORY HINTS

1. Avoid inconsistency.
2. Always give employees a chance to explain their action before taking disciplinary action. Don't allow too much time for a "cooling off" period before disciplining an employee.
3. Be specific in your criticisms.
4. Delegate responsibility wisely.
5. Do not argue or lose your temper, and avoid being impatient.
6. Promote mutual respect and be fair, impartial, and open-minded.
7. Keep in mind that asking for employees' advice and input can be helpful in decision making.
8. If you make promises, keep them.
9. Always keep the feelings, abilities, dignity and motives of your staff in mind.
10. Remain loyal to your employees' interests.
11. Never criticize employees in front of others, or treat employees like children.
12. Admit mistakes. Don't place blame on your employees, or make excuses.
13. Be reasonable in your expectations, give complete instructions, and establish well-planned goals.
14. Be knowledgeable about office details and procedures, but avoid becoming bogged down in details.
15. Avoid supervising too closely or too loosely. Employees should also view you as an approachable supervisor.
16. Remember that employees' personal problems may affect job performance, but become involved only when appropriate.
17. Work to develop workers, and to instill a feeling of cooperation while working toward mutual goals.
18. Do not overpraise or underpraise, be properly appreciative.
19. Never ask an employee to discipline someone for you.
20. A complaint, even if unjustified, should be taken seriously.

NOTES

BASIC FUNDAMENTALS OF SPORTS

CONTENTS

	Page
PRINCIPLES OF ATHLETICS	1
BASKETBALL	1
CROSS-COUNTRY AND DISTANCE RUNNING	4
SOCCER	8
SOFTBALL	11
SPEEDBALL	14
TOUCH FOOTBALL	18
VOLLEYBALL	23

BASIC FUNDAMENTALS OF SPORTS

PRINCIPLES OF ATHLETICS

ATHLETICS IN THE PHYSICAL TRAINING PROGRAM

- ❖ Athletics deserve a prominent place in the physical training program because they contribute to the increased efficiency of the student. Because of the competitive nature of athletics and their natural appeal, the students take part in them with enthusiasm. Athletic teams formed at the intramural and higher levels are a strong unifying influence and provide one of the best means of developing esprit de corps.

- ❖ The athletic sports selected must be vigorous to insure good conditioning value.

- ❖ All the components of physical fitness cannot be developed with athletics alone. These sports are beneficial primarily in sustaining interest in the program and maintaining a level of physical fitness. Therefore, athletics are to be considered as a supplement and not a substitute for the less interest conditioning drills.

BASKETBALL

INTRODUCTION
Basketball has enjoyed increased popularity and growth within the past few years, unequaled by any other American sport. It should be comparatively easy for an instructor to create interest in basketball among student personnel, both for conditioning and recreational purposes. Few sports have the potentialities that basketball has for developing coordination, endurance, skill, teamwork, and the will to win. It is an excellent activity for the sustaining stage. One of the objectives of a physical training program is 100 percent participation. A well-organized basketball program makes it possible to more nearly accomplish this objective than any other athletic activity.

BASIC SKILLS
Men prefer to play rather than practice so, whenever possible, a part of each instruction period should be devoted to a scrimmage game. To prevent the loss of program interest, the instructor should vary the practice routine, add new plays, organize tournaments, and devise other ways to maintain enthusiasm. He should use textbooks written by professional basketball coaches to plan and teach offensive and defensive plays.

    A. **Fundamentals**

        1. Shooting Baskets
            a. One-hand Set Shots: Shoot from a balanced position. Keep both feet on the floor. Follow through.
            b. Two-hand Set Shots: Shoot from a balanced position and apply equal pressure on the ball with each hand. Keep both feet on the floor. Follow through.

c. Lay-ups: Jump high, reach high before releasing the ball. Spin the ball, using the backboard when possible.
d. Shooting while on move. This is usually a one-handed shot. Shoot off opposite foot from the hand that releases the ball.
e. Jump Shot: Jump high, release ball with one hand at apex of height. Most common shot today.
f. Free Throws: These are one-hand and two-hand underhand throws and two-hand push shots. Put a slight back spin on the ball.

2. Ball-handling.
    a. Two-hand Chest Pass: Step in the direction of the pass. Use a wrist action to release the ball with a back spin.
    b. One-hand and Two-hand Bounce Pass: Step in the direction of the pass. Bounce the ball a reasonable distance in front of the receiver, putting a back spin on the ball with a wrist action.
    c. One-hand Baseball Pass: Step in the direction of the pass; throw as you would throw a baseball. This is used mostly for long passes.
    d. Two-hand Overhead Pass: Hold the ball above the head with the arms extended. Throw with a wrist action. This pass is used mainly to get the ball to the pivot man who is close to the basket.

3. Dribbling
    a. Changing Hand With Ball: Only one hand may touch the ball at one time while dribbling. The hand may be alternated.
    b. Change of Pace: Changing speed and direction while dribbling.
    c. Dribbling Exercise With Eyes Not Directly On Ball: Change direction; change hand; keep the head up with the eyes directed toward possible passing or shooting situations.

4. Footwork
    a. Pivoting: Give the pivotman or center special practice in pivoting. One foot remains stationary while the opposite foot is mobile.
    b. Individual Defense: Stress footwork and the position of the hands and body.
    c. Check Position of Feet When Shooting Various Types of Shots: Points to check: the position of balance; correct foot forward when in shooting position; the distance between each foot.

B. Small Group or Team Practice

1. Man-to-Man Defense
    a. Switching: Each defensive man is responsible for defending against a designated man, until a screen or block forces the defensive man to change defensive responsibility.
    b. Nonswitching: Each defensive man is responsible for a designated man with the defensive man going through or behind screens and blocks.

2. Man-to-man Offense: Various types of offensive formations have been especially designed to combat man-to-man defense. Use textbooks written by professional coaches for technical knowledge.

3. **Zone Defense:** There are numerous variations of this type defense aimed at defending a restricted area in front of the basket. The defensive target is the ball, not the man.

4. **Zone Offense:** The zone offense forces the defense to adjust position, as a unit, rapidly and often. Zone offense is most effective when employing rapid movement of the ball within the defense area.

5. **Defense Against Fast Break:** Stress rebound work on the offensive backboard. Stress court balance by offensive team.

6. **Fast Break Offense:** Move down court into scoring or offensive territory quickly.

PRACTICE DRILLS

Some practice routines are:

A. **Keep-Away:** Divide unit into two groups. Designate each individual's defensive responsibility by name or number. Use half of a basketball court as the playing area. The team in possession of the ball passes it among the team members until the defense gets possession of it. Basketball rules apply. Continue with each team taking turns as it gets possession of the ball.

B. **Shooting Exercise:** Divide unit into small groups. Each group has a ball. Designate the various positions on the floor where the shooting practice is to be done. Use a pre-arranged scoring method. Play numerous games, giving each group an opportunity to shoot from all positions on the floor.

C. **Dribbling Exercise:** Divide unit into two or three groups. Each group has a ball. Conduct a dribbling relay. Place obstacles for dribblers to avoid and designate the path each team will follow.

D. **Defense Exercises:** Use the two free throw circles and the restraining circle at center court. Place five men around the outside of each circle. One man is in the center of each ring. It is the job of the man in the center to intercept or deflect the path of the ball which is passed from man to man in the circle. When the man inside the circle succeeds in intercepting, deflecting, or touching the ball, the passer takes his place.

FACILITIES AND EQUIPMENT

A. **Facilities:** In some sections of the country, outdoor facilities may be used, and they are easily constructed. The minimum dimensions of a court for competition are approximately 74 feet by 42 feet; maximum dimensions are 94 feet by 50 feet.

B. **Equipment:** A basketball is the only required equipment. For highly organized competition, however, uniforms, special shoes, and other equipment may be required.

RULES

So-called college rules or, more correctly, The National Collegiate Athletic Association rules, are used in conducting basketball in the physical training program. Each year a new paper-bound guide booklet is published and sold by the NCAA.

CROSS-COUNTRY AND DISTANCE RUNNING

INTRODUCTION

A. Long-distance running gives some benefits that cannot be obtained in the same degree from any other sport. It builds powerful leg muscles, increases the long capacity, and develops endurance. For these reasons, cross-country and distance running should be included in the physical training program. These sports require only a few miles of open space that is available at school. They do require time, however, and many physical training supervisors do not find it feasible to use them as individual full-time sports. Short cross-country runs and middle-distance runs can be used to supplement other activities, particularly the team sports or the sports that develop precision or agility rather than endurance. Short cross-country runs can be scheduled once a week, gradually increasing the distance as the physical condition of the men improves; or distance running can be combined with other activities such as the conditioning exercises.

B. Cross-country and the distance runs do not enjoy equal popularity with other sports, for obvious reasons. They require great endurance, and endurance requires months of rigid training. There is a common belief that long-distance running is too strenuous, often resulting in permanent injury to the heart. While distance running may be harmful to the man who overdoses the sport, when he is not in proper physical condition, the conditioned, supervised distance runner is in no greater danger of strain than the man engaged in any other athletic activity.

LONG-DISTANCE RUNS

Any run over a mile is classified as a long-distance run. The instructor may vary the distance of the run during the season, or he may standardize it at whatever length will best suit his men or the facilities available to him. Two miles is the most popular distance. Often, the two-mile run is included as an event in track and field meets, but more frequently it is treated as a separate sport. The two-mile run may be run on any type of flat outdoor course, on a regular cinder track, or on a grass or dirt course. Because the ground is often frozen too hard for long-distance running during cold weather, the two-mile run is not recommended as a winter activity except in mild climates. The sport is too strenuous for very hot weather. The run cannot be held indoors. Constant pounding of the feet on the hard surface causes shin splints and injuries to the ankle joints.

CROSS-COUNTRY RUNS

Cross-country is a distance run held on a course laid out along roads, across fields, over hills, through woods, on any irregular ground. A flat cylinder or dirt track is not a suitable surface for cross-country running. Opinions vary as to the proper length of a cross-country course. Some runs are as long as six miles. Five miles used to be accepted as standard, but recently there has been a tendency to shorten the run to four or even three miles. Only if time is available for a full-season cross-country program should the physical training instructor try to train men for a five-mile course. If time is limited, or if cross-country running is being used to supplement other activities, the three-mile course is long enough for most men.

PLACE IN THE PROGRAM

Cross-country and distance running should be used only after the men reach the sustaining stage of conditioning. They should then be scheduled occasionally to provide variety in the program. Cross-country running has the advantage of allowing mass participation. Interest can be stimulated by putting the runs on a competitive basis.

BASIC SKILLS

A. Cross-Country Running Form: Running form in cross-country races varies with the terrain and the contour of the course. On the flat, use the same form as used in a two-mile run. The body lean should be between 5 and 10 percent. A lean of more than 10 percent places too much weight and strain on the legs. A lean of less than 5 percent is retarding. In running uphill, lean forward at a greater angle and cut the length of the stride. To gain an added lift, swing the arms high and bring the knees up high on each stride. Do not slow down after reaching the crest of the hill, but resume the flat course stride as soon as the ground levels off. The runner's stride will naturally lengthen in doing downhill, but he should not stretch his stride or increase his pace too much. There is less control and less balance when running downhill; therefore, there is greater danger of turning an ankle and of falling. Keep the arms low, swinging freely, and use them as a brake and as a balance. Coming onto the flat from a downhill run, do not slow down but float or coast into a flat course pace. More energy will be used in attempting to brake the speed of descent than in maintaining the faster pace and slowing down gradually. Run on the toes or the balls of the feet, rather than on the heels. Landing on the heels throughout a five-mile course would jolt the entire body injuriously. Runners who have a tendency to strike the heel on the ground should wear a cotton or sponge rubber pad in the heels of their shoes, unless their footgear has rubber heels.

B. Racing Tactics for Cross-Country

1. Teams can be pitted against each other in cross-country races. Certain members of the team may need encouragement along the way. If the team runs well-bunched for most of the course, the stronger runners can lead and encourage the weaker men. The pace should be scaled to the pace of the average runner on the team. Within a mile of the finish, however, the group should break and each man run out the race for himself.

2. If the coach prefers his team to run on an individual basis, there are several techniques for outwitting opponents. A good runner may not take the lead but stay behind an opponent and conserve his energy for the final sprint. The opponent may tire himself out trying to maintain the lead and become so discouraged when passed by a strong sprint near the finish line that he will not fight to reach the tape first. If leading an opponent, a runner may discourage him by constantly increasing the lead when he is out of sight. Opportunities for doing this frequently occur at corners of the course obscured by trees or bushes. If the leading runner sprints a short distance after rounding the corner, he may increase his lead 10 or 15 yards. After this has happened two or three times, an easily discouraged opponent may cease to be a serious contender for the race.

PRACTICE METHODS

A. Conditioning is more essential to distance and cross-country running than to any other sport. Championship distance running depends on stamina, and stamina can be developed only through constant training. A man of only average ability can become an outstanding distance runner by steady and careful training. Hiking is the best method for getting into condition before the season opens. Long walks build up leg muscles. During the first month of the season, training should be gradual, starting with short distances and increasing day by day. At first, the legs will become stiff, but the stiffness gradually disappears if running is practiced for a while every day. To prevent strain, it is essential to limber up thoroughly each day before running.

B. In the mass training of a large group, leaders should be stationed at the head and the rear of the column, and they should make every effort to keep the men together. After determining the abilities of the men in cross-country running, it is advisable to divide the unit into three groups. The poorest conditioned group is started first, the best conditioned group last. The starting time of the groups should be staggered so that all of them come in about the same time. In preliminary training, the running is similar to ordinary road work in that it begins with rather slow jogging, alternating with walking. The speed and distance of the run is gradually increased. As the condition of the men improves, occasional sprints may be introduced. At first, the distance run is from one-half to one mile. It is gradually increased to two or three miles. On completing the run, the men should be required to continue walking for three or four minutes before stopping, to permit a gradual cooling off and return to normal physiological functioning.

FACILITIES AND EQUIPMENT

A. A course three or five miles long should be measured and marked by one or the three methods specified below:

   1. Directional arrows fastened to the top of a tall post and placed at every point where the course turns. Such signs should also be placed at ever other point where there may be doubt as to the direction of travel.

   2. A lime line placed on the ground over the entire course.

   3. Flags: they should be clearly visible to the runners.
      a. A red flag indicates a left turn.
      b. A white flag indicates a right turn.
      c. A blue flag indicates the course is straight ahead.

B. There should be at least one stopwatch (preferably three) for timing the runners.

RULES

A. Team Members: A cross-country team shall consist of seven men, unless otherwise agreed. In dual meets, a maximum of twelve men may be entered, but a maximum of seven shall enter into the scoring.

B. Scoring: First place shall score 1 point, second place 2, third place 3, and so on. All men who finish the course shall be ranked and tallied in this manner. The team score shall then be determined by totaling the points scored by the first five men of each team to finish. The team scoring the least number of points shall be the winner. Note: Although the sixth and seventh runners of a team to finish do not score points toward their team's total, it should be noted that their places, if better than those of any of the first five of an opposing team, serve to increase the team score of the opponents.

C. Cancellation of Points: If less than five (or the number determined prior to the race) finish, the places of all members of that team shall be disregarded.

D. Tie Event: In case the total points scored by two or more teams result in a tie, the event shall be called a tie.

SOCCER

INTRODUCTION

A. Soccer is one of the best athletic activities for developing endurance, agility, leg strength, and a great degree of skill in using the legs. The game is the most popular sport in Europe and is the national game of many of the Central and South American countries. In recent years, it has become popular in United States schools and colleges.

B. A soccer ball is the only equipment needed for the game, and the men can learn to play it easily. The men do not need much skill to participate, but the amount they can developed in unlimited.

PLACE IN THE PROGRAM

Soccer should be introduced into the physical training program during the latter part of the slow improvement stage and used as a competitive activity in the sustaining stage. It is primarily a spring or fall sport. Any level field is suitable for competition. The boundaries for the soccer field are similar to the dimensions for a football field. Goal posts are essential to the game, but they are easily constructed and are usually of a temporary nature, so that they may be removed when not in use.

BASIC SKILLS

A. Passing: Passing with the feet is the basic means of moving the ball. Short passes are easier to control and can be done more accurately than long ones. Emphasis should be continually placed on skill in passing.

B. Dribbling: The ball is dribbled by a series of kicks with the inside or outside of the foot. Do not kick with the toe. Keep the head over the ball when kicking and propel it only a short distance at a time. Keep it close to the feet. When the ball gets very far from the feet while dribbling, an opposing player can easily take it away.

C. Instep Kicking: The instep kick, which is the basic soccer kick, is made from the knee joint instead of from the hip as in football. The toe does not come in contact with the ball. It is pointed downward and the instep (the shoe laces) is applied to the ball with a vigorous snap from the knee. For a stationary ball, the non-kicking foot is alongside the ball at the time of the kick. For a ball rolling toward the kicker, his non-kicking foot stops short of the ball; for a ball rolling away from the kicker, his non-kicking foot stops beyond the ball. The kicker must keep his eye on the ball until it has left his foot.

D. Inside-of-the-Foot Kicking: The ball is kicked with the inside of the foot and the leg is swung from the hip. The toe is turned outward and the sole of the foot is parallel with the ground as the foot strikes the ball. The tall should be well under the body at the time of contact. This kick is used for short passes and for dribbling.

E. Foot Trapping: The foot trap is the method of stopping the ball by trapping it between the ground and the foot. Place the sole of the foot on top of the ball at the instant it touches the ground, but do not stamp on it. Keep the foot relaxed. This is an effective way to stop a high-flying ball.

F. Shin Trapping: The shin trap is a method of stopping the ball with the shins. Stand just forward of the spot where the ball should strike the ground and allow it to strike the shins in flight or on the bounce. Use either one or both legs from the knee down, but do not allow the ball to strike the toe.

G. Body Trapping: The body trap is another method of gaining control of a ball in flight. Intercept the ball with any part of the upper body except the arms and hands. Keep the body relaxed and inclined toward the ball. To keep the ball from bouncing, move backward from it as it strikes the body. This will drop the ball at the feet in position for dribbling or passing.

H. Heading: Heading is the technique for changing the direction of the flight of a ball by butting it with the head. Tense the neck muscles and jump up to meet the ball. Butt the ball with the forehead at about the hairline to reverse its direction; use the side of the head to deflect it to the side. Always watch the ball, even during contact.

OFFENSIVE AND DEFENSIVE POSITIONS

The forwards usually play on the offensive half of the field and remain in a W formation. The fullbacks usually play on the defensive half of the field. The halfbacks are the backbone of the team; they move forward on the offense and back on defense. The goal keeper almost always remains within a few feet of the goal.

DRILLS TO DEVELOP BASIC SKILLS

Several skills are recommended to develop skill in kicking, passing, and shooting. The circle formation may be used for training in any of the basic skills. The ball may be headed or trapped as it is moved around or across the circle.

ABRIDGED RULES

A. A soccer team is composed of eleven players.

B. The player propels the ball by kicking it with the feet or any part of the legs, by butting it with his head, and by hitting it with any portion of his body except his arms or hands.

C. The goalkeeper is the only man allowed to use his hands on the ball, but he may only handle the ball in the goalkeeper's area. The term hands includes the whole arm from the point of the shoulder down.

D. A goal is made by causing the ball to cross completely the section of the goal line lying between the uprights and under the cross bar.

E. Each goal scores one point for the team scoring the goal.

F. The penalty for a foul committed anywhere on the playing field (except by the defensive team in its penalty area) is a free kick awarded to the team that committed the foul.

G. All opponents must be at least 10 yards from the ball when a free kick is taken.

H. The penalty for a foul committed by the defensive team in its penalty area is a penalty kick.

I. A penalty kick is a free kick at the goal from the spot 12 yards directly in front of the goal. The only players allowed within the penalty area at the time of the kick are the kicker and the defending goalkeeper.

J. An official game consists of four quarters.

K. Teams change goals at the end of every quarter.

L. In the event of a tie, an extra quarter is played.

M. After a ball has crossed a side line and has been declared out of play, it is put back into play by a free kick from the side line by a member of the team opposing the team that caused the ball to be out of bounds. The kick is taken from the point at which the ball crosses the side line as it goes out of bounds.

N. When the offensive team causes the ball to go behind the opposing team's goal line, excluding the portion between the goal posts, the opposing team is awarded a goal kick—a free kick taken within the goal area that must come out of the penalty area to be in play.

O. When the defensive team causes the ball to go behind its own goal line, excluding the portion between the goal posts, the opposing team is awarded a corner kick—a free kick taken by a member of the offensive team at the quarter circle at the corner flag-post nearest to where the ball went behind the goal line. The flat-post must not be removed.

P. The game is started and, after a goal has been scored, is resumed by placing the ball in the center of the mid-field line. Players must be on their side of the line until the ball is kicked. The ball must be kicked forward and must move a least two feet to be legal. The first kicker may not touch the ball twice in succession at the kick-off. The opposing team must be ten yards from the ball until it moves.

11

SOFTBALL

INTRODUCTION

A. Softball is a game that is known in every corner of the country and has become a familiar sight in every sandlot in America. During and since World War II, it has become one of the principal physical training activities.

B. Softball is patterned after baseball, but has different advantages because it requires less equipment and is easily adapted to every age group. It requires a smaller play area; the ball is larger and softer; and the bats are lighter, making them easier to handle. Because of its popularity, a majority of our young people have a general understanding of softball and softball rules, but only a comparative few possess the skill and knowledge to obtain the maximum benefit and satisfaction from the game

PLACE IN THE PROGRAM

A. Softball is a sustaining type of activity. It does not require continuous exertion on the part of each player; however, it is an enjoyable and occasionally strenuous game that should be included in the physical training program.

B. When a group already knows something about pitching, fielding, and batting, the instructor should give only a brief review of these fundamental skills, but place more emphasis on the rules and offensive and defensive strategy. Most of the time devoted to softball should be used for organized competition.

ORGANIZATION OF INSTRUCTION

When instruction is given on the basic skills and techniques, the students should first be shown the correct method of executing each skill. The class should then be divided into groups to practice. Ample time should be provided to familiarize each individual with the technique of playing each position as well as the basic skills necessary to play every position. When this instruction is completed, the class should be divided into teams for organized competition.

BASIC SKILLS

A. Batting: Select a bat that balances easily—hands grasp the handle at a point where the butt is neither too heavy nor too light. For a right-handed batter, the left foot points at about a 45° angle toward the pitcher, and the right foot points toward homeplate. The feet are about 8 inches apart. The head and eyes face the pitcher, and the bat is over the right shoulder, hands away from the body. The batting position is slightly to the rear of the center of the plate. In swinging, keep the eyes on the ball, twisting at the waist. As a result of the twist, the arms will swing automatically. The power of the swing is developed with a snap of the wrists and the extension of the arms in the follow-through.

B. Bunting: The stance for bunting is the same as for batting. When the ball leaves the pitcher's hand, immediately bring the bat from over the shoulder, moving the right hand slightly up the handle, until the bat is directly over the plate. Rotate the body so that it faces the pitcher. The feet are comfortably apart. Meet the ball squarely, absorbing the shock with the arms. Hold the edge of the bat perpendicular to the direction in which the ball is to be bunted.

C. Base Running: Upon hitting the ball, the runner must start quickly without watching where the ball goes. He should get to the first base as fast as possible and be ready to continue running at the coach's direction. Speed is the most important factor, but running the shortest distance between bases is also essential.

D. Sliding: Use the hook slide going into the base, with the body relaxed, extending either foot in a sweeping motion, touching the toe to the bag.

E. Catching: Assume the knee bend position, with the upper arms parallel to the ground, forearms vertical and palms down. As the ball strikes the mitt, grasp it with the bare hand. On high pitches, cup the fingers of the bare hand to prevent injury. On low pitches, extend the palms toward the pitcher with the thumbs down. Always avoid pointing the fingers toward the pitcher. The catcher must not sacrifice accuracy for speed in throwing to bases and must learn through experience when he can throw a player out at base.

F. Pitching: Pitching, to a large degree, determines a team's defensive strength, and pitching can only be developed through practice. To hold the ball, grasp it loosely with the fingers, the index, middle, and third finger on one side and the thumb and fourth finger on the other side. The most effective manner of pitching is the windmill pitch. To start the wind-up, face the homeplate with both feet on the rubber. The ball is held in front with both hands. Raise the left foot to the rear as the right arm swings backward. The body pivots to the right, the left hand is extended and balances the motion, and the head and eyes remain on the catcher's glove. When the right arm reaches the nine o'clock position, step forward with the left foot directly toward homeplate, swing the arm forward, and twist the body to the left. With a snap of the wrist on the underhand swing, release the ball and follow through. Control is very important and must be gained through practice.

G. Infield Playing: An infielder must anticipate at all times what he should do in case he has to play the ball. On batted ground balls, he should play the ball to his front. Field each ground ball with the feet apart, hands well out in front. When the ball strikes the glove, secure it with the bare hand. The hands and arms should relax, and the arms should be drawn backward toward the right hip preparatory to the throw.

H. Outfield Playing: An outfielder should be alert and fast and able to judge the ball so he can get in the best position to catch it. It takes practice to become a successful fielder. To catch a fly ball, he extends the arms forward, forming a cup with the hands. He keeps his eyes on the ball until he has firm possession of it. He catches ground balls in the same way as the infielder (see G above).

DRILLS

A. Pitching and Catching: Divide the class into two lines fifty feet apart; one side will pitch, the other will catch. Make corrections on form for both pitching and catching. emphasize form and control. Change over.

B. Infield Play: Divide the class into seven-man groups. Place each group in a separate area, simulating (if necessary) the softball diamond. Designate a first, second, and third baseman, and a shortstop. Choose one man to hit balls and one to catch at homeplate. The player who hits balls first calls a play such as first base, double play, throw it home, etc. He then hits a ground ball to one of the infielders who, in turn, carries out the prescribed play. Demand enthusiasm and hustle. Change over occasionally and allow each man to play each position.

C. Outfield Play: Place seven men in the outfield, but do not designate definite positions. Have a player hit both fly and ground balls to the field. Use one player to catch balls at homeplate. After each ball has been played, have it relayed back to the hitter. Change positions so that each player has an opportunity to play in the outfield.

D. Base Running: Divide the class into fifteen-man groups. Time each runner in a complete circuit of bases. Stimulate competition. Critique each runner.

E. Hitting and Bunting: Divide the class into regular nine-man teams. Place one team in the infield to shag balls. The players on the other team take turns at bat, hitting ten balls each. On the last pitch, they lay down a bunt and run to first base, trying to beat the throw. Change over.

OFFENSIVE AND DEFENSIVE STRATEGY

A. Offensive: Hit only good balls (balls in the strike zone). Runners should run out fly balls at top speed, in case the ball is dropped or an error is committed. There is a better possibility of stealing a base than of the next batter hitting safely. Do not hesitate in stealing. Do not attempt to steal third base when two men are out, because a runner should be able to score from second base on a hit or on an error. It is best to attempt to steal second base with two outs. With no outs and runners on first and second base, a bunt combined with a double steal is good strategy. A runner can usually score from third base on a fly ball or on an error.

B. Defensive: A play should always back up another player receiving a throw at a base, or a player attempting to make a play on a fly or ground ball. The player who is nearest the ball should call for it and make the catch or play. Each player should be aware of the situation and know exactly what to do if he receives the ball. Receive bunts, flys, and ground balls with both hands. Have firm possession of the ball before attempting a throw. On force plays, do not stand on the base. It is better to make certain of one out, rather than risk an error in trying for a double play. When a shorter throw can put a runner out at base, it is best to attempt the shorter throw. With runners on first and second base, it is better to force out at third than to try a double play from second to first base. An outfielder should throw the ball directly to the spot where the play is likely to be made, unless it is a long fly and a relay appears to be quicker.

SPEEDBALL

INTRODUCTION AND GENERAL DESCRIPTION

Speedball is a game that offers vigorous and varied action with plenty of scoring opportunities. It is easy to learn and provides spontaneous fun. Little equipment is needed—a ball is all that is absolutely necessary. Speedball combines the kicking, trapping, and intercepting elements of soccer; the passing game of basketball; and the punting, drop-kicking, and scoring pass of football. Two teams of eleven men each play the game under official rules, but any number of players may successfully constitute a team. An inflated leather ball, usually a soccer ball, is used. The playing field is a football field with a football goal post at each end. The game starts with a soccer-type kickoff. The kicking team tries to retain possession of the ball and advance it toward the opposite goal by passing or kicking it. Running with the ball is not allowed, so there is no tackling or interference. When the ball touches the ground, it cannot be picked up with the hands or caught on the bounce, but must be played as in soccer until it is raised into the air directly from a kick; then the hands are again eligible for use. When the ball goes out of bounds over the side lines, it is given to a player of the team opposite that forcing the ball out, and is put into play with a basketball throw-in; when it goes over the end line without a score, it is given to a player of the opposing team who may either pass or kick it onto the field. When two opposing players are contesting the possession of a held ball, the official tosses the ball up between them as in basketball. Points are scored by kicking the ball under the crossbar of the goal posts, drop-kicking the ball over the crossbar, completing a forward pass into the end zone for a touchdown, or by kicking the ball under the crossbar of the goal posts on a penalty kick.

PLACE IN THE PROGRAM

Speedball, like soccer, should be introduced into the physical training program during the latter part of the toughening stage and used as a competitive activity in the sustaining stage. It may be played any time the weather permits, but it is primarily a spring or fall activity.

BASIC SKILLS

    A. Soccer Techniques
        1. Kicking
        2. Passing
        3. Heading
        4. Trapping

    B. Football Techniques
        1. Punting
        2. Drop-kicking
        3. Forward passing

    C. Basketball Techniques
        1. Passing
        2. Receiving
        3. Pivoting

    D. Kickups and Lifts: The kickup is a play in which the player lifts the ball into the air with his feet so that he may legally play the ball with his hands. The kickup is generally used to make the transition from ground play to aerial play. The technique of making the play depends upon whether the ball is rolling or stationary. To kick up a ball rolling or bouncing toward the player, the foot is held on the ground with the toe drawn down until the ball rolls onto the foot, then the foot is raised, projecting the ball upward. If the ball is stationary, the player rolls it backward with one foot, then places the foot where the ball will roll onto it. He can then lift the ball with that foot. If a ball is running away from the player, he should stop it with a foot and play it as a stationary ball. There is also a method of raising the ball by standing over it with a foot on either side. He presses his feet against the ball and jumps into the air, propelling the ball into his hands.

OFFENSIVE POSITIONS AND STRATEGY

The positions of the players in speedball are much the same as in soccer. However, some of the positions are designated by different names. There are eleven players on each team. The forward line is composed of five players: the right end, right forward, center, left forward, and left end. The second line consists of right halfback, fullback, and left halfback. In the next line is the right guard and left guard. The player who defends the goal is the goal guard. The strategy employed in speedball during offensive play is very similar to that of soccer.

DEFENSIVE PLAY

There are two types of defensive formations in speedball: man-for-man and position defense. Man-for-man defense is recommended for beginning players.

ABRIDGED RULES

A. The Field: 360 feet long and 160 feet wide (a regulation football field).

B. Players: Eleven on a team. The goal guard has no special privileges.

C. Time: Ten-minute quarters, two minutes between. Ten minutes between halves. Five minutes for extra overtime periods. (Begin first overtime by a jump ball (see G.3. below) at center, same goals; change goals in the event of a second overtime period.)

D. Winner of Toss: The winner of the toss has the choice of kicking, receiving, or defending a specific goal.

E. Starting Second and Fourth Quarters: The ball is given to the team that had possession at the end of the previous quarter, out of bounds, as in basketball.

F. Half: The team that received at the start of the first half kicks off at the beginning of the second half.

G. The Game: The game is started with a kickoff from the middle line (50-yard line), both teams being required to remain back of their respective restraining lines until the ball is kicked. The ball must travel forward.

1. The most characteristic feature of the playing rules of speedball is the differentiation between a fly ball (or aerial ball) and a ground ball. A player is not permitted to touch a ground ball with his hands and must play it as in soccer. A fly ball is one that has risen into the air directly from the foot of a player (example: punt, drop-kick, place-kick, or kickup). Such a ball may be caught with the hands

provided the catch is made before the ball strikes the ground again. A kickup is a ball that is so kicked by a player that he can catch it himself. A bounce from the ground may not be touched with the hand because it has touched the ground since being kicked. This rule prohibits thee ordinary basketball dribble, but one overhead dribble (throwing the ball into the air and advancing to catch it before it hits the ground) is permitted.

2. If a team causes the ball to go out of bounds over the side lines, a free thrown-in (any style) is given to the opposing team. When the ball goes over the end line without scoring, it is given to the opponents who may pass or kick from out of bounds at that point.

3. In case two players are contesting the possession of a held ball, even in the end zone, a tie ball is declared and the ball is tossed up between them.

4. The kick-off is made from any place on or behind the 50-yard line. Team A (the kicking team) must be behind the ball when it is kicked. Team B must stay back of its restraining line (ten yards' distance) until the ball is kicked (penalty—a violation). The ball must go forward before A may play it (penalty—violation). Kick off out of bounds to opponents at that spot. A kick-off touched by B and going out of bounds, no impetus added, still belongs to B. A kick-off, in possession and control of B and then fumbled out of bounds, belongs to A at that spot. A field goal from kick-off (under crossbar, etc.) scores 3 points.

H. Scoring Methods

1. Field Goal (3 points): A soccer-type kick, in which a ground ball is kicked under the crossbar and between the goal posts from the field of play or end zone. (A punt going straight through is not a field goal for it is not a ground ball. The ball must hit the ground first.). A drop-kick from the field of play that goes under a crossbar does not count as a field goal. A drop-kick from the end zone that goes under the crossbar counts as a field goal; if it goes over the crossbar, it is ruled as a touch back.

2. Drop-kick (2 points): A scoring drop-kick must be made from the field of play and go over the crossbar and between the uprights. The ball must hit the ground before it is kicked (usually with the instep).

3. End Goal (1 point): This is a ground ball which receives its impetus (kicked or legally propelled by the body) from any player, offensive or defensive, in the end zone and passes over the end line but not between the goal posts.

4. Penalty Kick (1 point): This is a ball kicked from the penalty mark that goes between the goal posts and under the crossbar. The penalty mark is placed directly in front of the goal at the center of the goal line.

5. Touchdown (1 point): A touchdown is a forward pass from the field of play completed in the end zone. The player must be entirely in the end zone. If he is on the goal line or has one foot in the field of play and the other in the end zone, the ball is declared out of bounds. If a forward pass is missed, the ball continues in

play but must be returned to the field of play before another forward pass or drop-kick may be made.

I. Substitutions: Substitutions may be made any time when the ball is not in play. If a player is withdrawn, he may not return during that same period.

J. Time Out: Three legal time-outs of two minutes each are permitted each team during the game.

K. Fouls

1. Personal (four disqualify): Kicking, tripping, charging, pushing, holding, blocking, or unnecessary roughness of any kind, such as running into an opponent from behind. Kicking at a fly ball and thereby kicking an opponent.

2. Technical: Illegal substitution, more than three time-outs in a game, unsportsmanlike conduct, unnecessarily delaying the game.

3. Violation: Traveling with the ball, touching a ground ball with the hands or arms, double overhead dribble, violating tie ball, and kicking or kneeing a fly ball before catching it.

4. Penalties: (The offended player shall attempt the kick.)

	Penalty	Location
Personal	In field of play	1 kick with no follow-up
Technical	In field of play	1 kick with no follow-up
Violation	In field of play	Out of bounds to opponent
Personal	In end zone	2 kick with no follow-up on last kick
Technical	In end zone	1 kick with no follow-up
Violation	In end zone	1 kick with no follow-up

l. Summary of Fouls

1. Fouls in the field of play allow no follow-up while fouls in the end zone always allow follow-up.

2. On penalty kicks, with no follow-up, only the kicker and goalie are involved.

3. On penalty kicks, with a follow-up, the kicking side is behind the ball and the defending side behind the end line or in the field of play. No one is allowed in the end zone or between the goal post except the goal guard. The kicker cannot play the ball again until after another player plays it, and he must make an actual attempt at goal.

TOUCH FOOTBALL

INTRODUCTION

Touch football has become a major active game on the lower levels of competition. Considering its similarity to football and yet its comparative simplicity, it is easy to understand the popularity of the game. The modification of regulation football rules for touch football eliminates the necessity for much special equipment, training, and professional leadership. Touch football encourages participation, reduces the number of injuries, and simplifies the teaching of fundamental rules, techniques, and skills.

PLACE IN THE PROGRAM

Touch football is an excellent conditioning activity, and it should be included in both the physical training and intramural programs. It may be used in the latter part of the toughening stage and during the sustaining stage of physical conditioning. It should be played in the fall when the interest in football is at its peak. Any level field can be used. Goal posts are desirable but not absolutely necessary.

ORGANIZATION OF INSTRUCTION

Most men know something about football, but not all have had an opportunity to play. Several short periods should be devoted to the instruction of all men in the basic fundamentals. A desirable method is to give five to ten minutes of instruction at the beginning of each football period and follow it by actual play.

BASIC SKILLS

   A. Offensive Stance: Touch football emphasizes speed; therefore, a high offensive stance should be used to facilitate a fast getaway. The feet should be about shoulder width apart and parallel, knees bent, thighs just above the horizontal and back nearly parallel with the ground. The head and eyes are up, and the right hand is extended straight downward, the fingers curled under, the thumb toward the rear. The left arm rests on the left thigh. There are many variations of this basic stance that may be used. The general principles are: Keep the feet spread for balance, the body under control, and the head up with the eyes on an opponent or the ball.

   B. Defensive Stance: This type stance may be similar to the offensive stance or somewhat higher to allow for better visibility and free use of the hands to ward off blockers. The same principles of balance, body control, and vision used in the offensive stance are applicable to the defensive stance.

   C. Blocking: Touch football rules do not permit the blocker to have both feet off the ground at the same time (flying block); therefore, the blocker should maintain a wide base for shoulder, upright, or cross-body blocks. For the shoulder block, the hands should be close to the chest, the elbows raised sideward, the feet under the body and widely spread, the head up, and the buttocks low. Upon contact, the feet should be moved rapidly in short, choppy steps to force the body forward, thus keeping the shoulder in contact with the opponent. The upright block is useful in the open field and is executed by the player while standing nearly erect. The feet are widely spread, knees slightly bent, the trunk inclined slightly forward, and the head erect. The arms are raised, and the hands are placed on the chest, forearms forward to contact the opponent. Due to the nature of the block, the opponent is contacted above the waist.

In performing the cross-body block, the blocker uses the hip to contact the opponent, usually in the area of the thighs. The execution of this type of block requires the blocker to throw his head, shoulders, and arms past the target area, thus bringing his hip into contact with his opponent. Then, assisted by movement of the hands and feet which are in contact with the ground, he forces the opponent backward or down. The shoulder, upright, or cross-body blocks may be used in the line or in the open field.

D. Ball Carrying: The first point to stress in ball carrying is the grip of the ball. The ball is placed in the arm with its long axis parallel to the forearm. It is held firmly and close to the body. The hand grips the lower point of the ball with the fingers spread to form a firm grip. It is difficult to teach the fine points of ball carrying in a few hours of instruction. Stress the principles. Teach runners to carry the ball in the arm away from the opponent. The runner should be cautioned to follow his interference and to keep his head up so he can avoid his opponents.

E. Forward Passing: Forward passing is one of the principal means of advancing the ball in touch football. Teach the method of gripping or holding the ball with the fingers spread on the laces and toward the end of the ball, cocking the arm with the hand holding the ball close to the head and the wrist rotated so that the rear point of the ball is pointing toward the head. The ball is delivered with a baseball catcher's peg motion, by extending the arm and imparting a spiral to the ball. To make a successful forward pass, it is usually best for the passer to have the feet spread comfortably and in contact with the ground, the free hand extended to aid the balance. He throws the ball to a spot where the receiver can catch it without breaking his stride. Do not allow beginners to attempt jump passes, as the successful throwing of this type of pass requires the skill of an experienced forward passer.

F. Pass Receiving: To catch a forward pass requires the receiver to keep his eyes on the ball, to run to the spot where he can reach the ball, to catch it without breaking stride, and to take it out of the air by relaxing the hands as the ball strikes. In receiving a pass over the shoulder, the little fingers are facing, with the thumbs outward and all fingers spread. In catching a pass while facing the passer, the receiver should catch a high pass with the thumbs facing and the little fingers out; and a low pass with the little fingers facing and the thumbs pointing outward.

DRILLS TO DEVELOP FUNDAMENTALS

It is recommended that the time available for instruction in the fundamentals be used in teaching the following skills: stance, shoulder block, cross-body block, forward passing, and pass receiving.

A. Stance Drill: Use the extended rectangular formation. Demonstrate the stance and tell the men they will execute the drill by the numbers. At the count of one, place the feet in position. At the count of two, bend the knees and trunk. At the count of three, lean forward and place one hand on the ground. After checking for errors and making corrections, command "UP" and execute the drill again. Have the men do this several times before progressing to the next drill.

B. Blocking Drills: All the blocks may be practiced by forming the class into two lines facing one another and having the men pair off. Explain the drill, demonstrate the block desired, and designate one line as blockers and the other as opponents. After several practice blocks, have the blockers become the opponents and the opponents become the blockers. During the course of the drill, emphasize the three phases of blocking: the approach, contact, and follow-through.

C. Forward Passing Drill: Form the class in groups of ten men each. The groups form two lines with the men about ten feet apart and the two lines ten to fifteen yards apart. Using at least one ball to a group, practice grip, balance, throwing with a spiral, and follow-through. The ball is thrown by each man, in turn, to the next man in the opposite line who catches it and throws.

D. Passing and Receiving Drill: Each of the groups is formed as for the drill outlined in C above. One man, the center, is stationed between the two files with the ball. One file is designated as passers and the other as receivers. The center snaps the ball to the first passer. He passes to the first receiver who runs down the field at the snap of the ball. The receiver catches the pass and returns the ball to the center. Upon his return, the receiver joins the "passer" file and the passer joins the "receiver" file. This rotation continues until all men have an opportunity to throw and receive forward passes.

E. Other Drills: If time permits, other fundamental drills may be included, such as snapping the ball from center, kicking, lateral passing, and other individual skills of a specialty nature.

OFFENSIVE FORMATIONS AND PLAY

A. A nine-man team is recommended. Three offensive formations are suggested for this size team. Of the three formations suggested, the double wing-back is the best.

B. To complete the instruction in offensive play, it will be necessary to insure that some member of the team can perform the individual specialties. These special skills are passing the ball from center, punting, free kicking for kick-offs, backfield pivots, handoffs, etc.

C. Men like to develop their own plays and should be encouraged to do so. Time must be made available for them to practice such plays before using them in a game.

DEFENSIVE PLAY

The class should be shown several defensive formations. Four different ones are applicable for the nine-man team. The selection of a defense depends upon the opponent's offense. The 4-2-2-1 and the 5-1-2-1 are better pass defense formations than the 4-3-2 and the 5-2-2. The latter formations are weak "down the middle." However, the 4-3-2 and 5-2-2 are stronger against a running attack. If fewer men are employed on a team, the defense could be altered by eliminating either linemen or backs, as required.

ORGANIZATION AND ADMINISTRATION

A. The instructor may divide the class into teams from the roster or by selecting team captains who, in turn, choose the remaining members of their teams.

B. The officials may be assistant instructors or selected individuals from the class. It is suggested that there should be at least one official for each game that is played.

Close supervision of play and strict enforcement of rules are necessary to prevent injuries from excessive roughness.

C. To insure the success of touch football in a physical training period, the teams should be organized into a class league to stimulate interest and competition, and to select the championship team.

D. There should be one ball for each fifteen men.

E. The area for practice and play should be grassed and level. The field should conform as nearly as possible to the size specified in paragraph 9.A.1.

RULES

It is important that the participants know the rules that govern touch football. It increases the players' enjoyment in the activity, lessens the chance of injury, and results in an organized contest. Official National Collegiate Athletic Association football rules shall govern all play except those special rules pertinent to touch football, as stated in the following subparagraphs.

A. Rule I: Field and Equipment
   1. Section 1 – Field: The game shall be played on a regulation football field with goal posts. When space is limited, the dimensions of the field may be reduced to 300 feet long by 120 feet wide.
   2. Section 2 – Uniforms: Distinctive jerseys, shorts, sweat suits, or trousers, and basketball shoes or regulation footwear may be worn. Pads, helmets, and cleated shoes are not authorized.

B. Rule II: Length of Game
   1. Section 1 – Periods: The game shall be played in four periods each ten minutes in length, with a one-minute interval between the first and second and the third and fourth periods; and with a ten-minute interval between the second and third periods.

   2. Section 2 – Contest: By mutual agreement of opposing coaches or captains, before the start of contest, the length of the periods may be shortened or lengthened.

   3. Section 3 – Time Out: Time out shall be taken
      a. After a touchdown, field goal, safety, or touch back.
      b. During a try for a point.
      c. After an incomplete forward pass.
      d. When the ball goes out of bounds.
      e. During the enforcement or declination of penalties.

C. Rule III: Players and Substitutes

   1. Section 1 – Players (nine-man team): Each team shall consist of nine players. The offensive team shall have a minimum of five players on the scrimmage line when the ball is snapped. Note: The following diagram designates the position of the players:

```
       END   GUARD       CENTER        GUARD   END
                      QUARTERBACK
                   HALFBACK   HALFBACK
                         FULLBACK
```

2. Section 2 – Players (six-man game): Each team shall consist of six players. The offensive team shall have a minimum of three players on the scrimmage line when the ball is snapped. Note: The following diagram designates the position of the players.

```
         END          CENTER          END
              HALFBACK   HALFBACK
                    FULLBACK
```

3. Section 3 – Substitutions: Unrestricted substitutions may be made when
   a. The ball is dead.
   b. The clock is running, provided substitutions are completed and the ball is snapped within 25 seconds after the ball is ready for play.

D. Rule IV: Playing Regulations

1. Section 1: Starting the game and putting ball in play after any score shall be as prescribed by the NCAA Football Rule Book, with exception of Rule 4, Sections 2 and 3.
2. Section 2 – Kick-off: The receiving team, in a nine-man game, shall have three players within five yards of its own restraining line until the ball is kicked.
3. Section 3 – Restriction: In a six-man game, the only restriction on the receiving team is that all players must remain back of their own restraining line until the ball is kicked.
4. Section 4 – Fumbled Ball: A ball that is fumbled and touches the ground during a run, kick, or lateral pass play, may not be advanced by either team. The ball may be touched and recovered by any player. It shall be dead and in possession of the player who first touches it after it strikes the ground.
   Note: Players shall be warned against diving on fumbled balls and may be penalized for unnecessary roughness.
5. Section 5 – Fumbled Ball or Lateral Pass: A fumbled ball or lateral pass, intercepted or recovered before it touches the ground, may be advanced by any player.
6. Section 6 – Downed Ball By Legal Touch: The player in possession of the ball is downed and the ball is dead when such player is touched by an opponent with both hands simultaneously above the waist and below the head.
7. Section 7 – Forward Passing: One forward pass may be made during each scrimmage play from behind the passer's scrimmage line.
8. Section 8 – Eligible Receivers: All players of offensive and defensive teams are eligible to receive forward passes. Two or more receives may successively touch a forward pass.

E. Rule V – Fouls and Penalties. Section 1 – Use of hands and arms. For both offense and defense, as prescribed in NCAA Football Rule Book.

VOLLEYBALL

INTRODUCTION

    A. Volleyball is a popular sport. The game entails much physical activity, yet it is not strenuous. It is, therefore, a game for young and older men alike, for beginners and for skilled players. It may be played indoors or outdoors on any type of terrain. As an informal activity, volleyball can be played by any number of men; as an organized activity, it provides, as few other sports do, a game for twelve men to play in a limited area.

    B. While volleyball requires no great skill to play, it does permit a high degree of proficiency. A man naturally gets more enjoyment when he knows the game and plays it well. For this reason, instruction in the basic skills should be provided.

ORGANIZATION

Usually a ten- to fifteen-minute period of instruction, followed by scrimmage during the first three or four classes is enough to teach the basic skills, rules, and techniques of volleyball. More time can be given to teaching basic skills, if available, but the emphasis is on competitive play rather than on formal instruction. It is best to lecture and demonstrate to the entire class, then divide the class into smaller groups for practice. For drills and scrimmages, divide the class so that there will be from twelve to twenty-four men to each court. One court may be used for instruction by allowing twelve players at a time to execute the drill while the other class members observe, act as coaches, or retrieve balls. After the instruction phase of training has been completed, divide the class into six-man teams. Organize the teams on the basis of ability. All teams should be as nearly equal as possible.

PLACE IN THE PROGRAM

Volleyball may be used occasionally as a competitive activity during the sustaining stage. It is a year-round sport, but it should be included in the physical training program only when it is impractical to conduct a more strenuous activity. It is an excellent self-interest activity.

    A. Passing
        1. Handling the Low Ball: A ball that is lower than the waist is one of the easiest to hit, but is also a frequent cause of the fouls of holding or carrying the ball. The best position for handling a low ball is to have the feet staggered, knees flexed, and arms flexed at the elbows and rotated so the thumbs are pointing outward, the palms up. When the fingers contact the ball, the entire body reacts in a lifting motion. The arms and hands swing upward in a scooping action. It is important that the fingers, not the palms, contact the ball, and that the ball is batted not thrown.

        2. Handling the High Ball: The chest pass is the most effective method of playing the ball. To receive the ball, the feet are staggered, knees are flexed, and the body is tilted forward. The elbows are raised sideward to a point in line with the shoulders. The wrists are extended in line with the forearm and the arms, wrists, and hands are rotated inward. To pass the ball, the hands are chest high, thumbs pointing inward. The fingers are flexed, forming a cup, allowing them to contact the ball. On contact with the ball, the wrists are snapped while the fingers and elbows are

pushed upward, sending the ball upward. A high ball is much easier to handle than a low one.

B. Serving
1. The Underhand Serve: Take a position behind the back line facing the net, left foot forward, holding the ball in the palm of the left hand. The left knee is flexed, the right knee is straight. Swing the right arm back and at the same time move the left hand (holding the ball) across the body in line with the right hip. Then swing the right arm forward hitting the ball off of the left hand with the palm of the right hand, raising the hips and arching the back in the same motion. Be certain to swing the right arm in a straight line, or the ball will be difficult to control.

2. Placement of the Serve: When the opposition is in formation, the server should try to place the ball in the right or left back area, and not near the net.

C. Setting It Up: A setup is a ball into the air near the net by one player, so a teammate may hit or "spike" it sharply downward into the opponent's court. The chest pass is the best pass to use. The ball is sent approximately ten feet into the air toward the spiker so it will descend from four to twenty inches from the net.

D. Spiking: The spike is a leap into the air and a sharp downward hitting of the ball into the opponent's court. A spiker must be able to spring easily from the floor, judge the movement of the ball, and strike it with a downward movement of his arm. To jump from the floor, step off with one foot and jump with the other. Stand with the right or left side to the net, facing the setup man. Much depends upon the setup man to place the ball in the proper position. The spiker jumps into the air and strikes the ball above its center so as to drive it downward. A snapping movement of the arm and wrist will drive the ball forward and downward with power and control. Aim for a weak spot in the opponent's defense.

E. Blocking: The block is a technique of defense used to prevent a spiker from driving the ball across the net. It is an attempt by one or more defensive players at the net to block a hard hit shot by using the force of the ball to send it immediately back into the opponent's court. An effective block is for forwards on the defensive team to spring into the air at the time of the spike, placing both hands and arms in the expected path of the ball. An effective block tends to upset the offense and presents another element for the spiker to worry about. To be effective, the blocker must anticipate the path of the ball and time his block with the spike.

DRILLS TO DEVELOP BASIC SKILLS

A. Passing
1. Divide the class into twenty-four-man groups. Have them form a circle and begin passing a ball around the circle trying to prevent it from touching the floor.

2. Divide each group with twelve men on a side facing the net. Form four ranks per side, with the first ranks passing the ball back and forth over the net until a pass is incomplete. Then have the second rank move up. Place the groups in a regular playing formation concentrating only on passing, using both the chest pass and the low pass.

B. Serving: Break the men into two groups—one line to act as servers, the other as retrievers. Change over frequently giving each man a chance. When the men can control the serve, have each server try to place the ball in the various areas of the court.

   C. Spiking: Have two lines on one side of the court facing the net. One line is the spiking line, the other is the setup line. One man from each line moves up to the net at one time. The spiker tosses to the setup, the setup sets the ball up for spiker, and the spiker drives it over the net. Rotate the lines.

OFFENSIVE PLAY

   A. Each member of a good offensive team should
      1. Be able to serve.
      2. Know the capabilities and weaknesses of each of his teammates.
      3. Have an understanding of all offensive plays.
      4. Be able to analyze the opponent's weaknesses.
      5. Always know what area of the court he is responsible for.
      6. Be ready to "back up" a teammate receiving the ball.

   B. The big offensive power is the spiker. It is also necessary, however, to build a well-balanced team that can serve, pass, and "set up."

DEFENSIVE PLAY

The reception and handling of serves and spikes is the primary duty of the team on defense.

   A. Receiving the Serve: The forwards move to the rear of their area. The left and right backs cover the rear, the center back plays slightly forward of the other two backs.

   B. Blocking: The block is made by the center forward and either the right or left forward. The forward not executing the block must cover the position left vacant.

ABRIDGED RULES

   A. The volleyball court is 30 feet wide by 60 feet long

   B. The top of the net is 8 feet high.

   C. A volleyball team consists of six players.

   D. A match consists of the best two out of three games.

   E. The first team scoring 15 points wins the game, provided that they have two points more than their opponents.

   F. A deuce game is a game in which both teams score 14 points. The game is continued until one team obtains a 2-point advantage over the other

   G. Only the serving team can score. If the serving team commits a fault, it loses the serve to the opposing team.

H. The team receiving the ball for service rotates one position in a clockwise direction.

I. The ball is put into play by serving from behind the back line.

J. A served ball touching the net results in the loss of the serve. At any other time during play, a ball touching the net is still in play.

K. The ball is out of play when it touches the ground or goes outside one of the boundary lines.

L. All line balls are good.

M. The players must hit or bat the ball; they may not throw, lift, or scoop it.

N. A player may not touch the ball with any part of the body below the knees.

O. A player may not play (touch) the ball twice in succession. In receiving a hard-driven spike, a defensive player may make several contacts with the ball even if they are not simultaneous. All such contacts, however, must constitute one continuous play, and all must be above the knees.

P. The ball may be touched no more than three times on one side of the net before being returned across the net to the opposing team.

Q. A player must not touch or reach across the net.

R. A player must not cross the line under the net; he may touch it, however.

S. For complete official volleyball rules, see the United States Volleyball Association: <u>Volleyball Official Guide</u>.

www.ingramcontent.com/pod-product-compliance
Lightning Source LLC
Chambersburg PA
CBHW080324020526
44117CB00035B/2644